The Western European Union and NATO

Building a European Defence Identity within the Context of Atlantic Solidarity

D1259088

BRASSEY'S ATLANTIC COMMENTARIES

Series Editor: **Eric Grove**

This new series will present a collection of introductory surveys of important issues affecting the Atlantic Alliance and its future. The booklets are written and edited with the general reader as well as the specialist in mind and are intended to provide necessary background knowledge for an informed and continuing debate on East-West and intra-Alliance relations. Among future titles planned are Spain's evolving role in NATO, the WEU and the EEC, and an assessment of the state of play on the future of burden-sharing and the transatlantic partnership. Other subjects to be covered will include regional security issues, political and economic topics, country studies and future perspectives for international security in the changing political environment of the 1990s.

Brassey's Atlantic Commentaries are produced in association with the NATO Information Service and various national Atlantic Committees or other associations and institutions concerned with different aspects of security. The opinions expressed here are the responsibility of the author and the editor and do not necessarily reflect the views of individual member governments of the WEU or NATO.

Brassey's Atlantic Commentaries No. 1

NATO's Defence of the North
Edited by Eric Grove

Titles of related interest from Brassey's

GROVE and WINDASS
The Crucible of Peace: Common Security in Europe

HANNING
NATO: Our Guarantee of Peace

GOLDSTEIN
Fighting Allies: Tensions within the Atlantic System

WINDASS
Avoiding Nuclear War: Commmon Security as a Strategy for the Defence of the West

BRASSEY'S ATLANTIC COMMENTARIES No. 2

THE WESTERN EUROPEAN UNION AND NATO

Building a European Defence Identity within
the Context of Atlantic Solidarity

ALFRED CAHEN

Belgian Ambassador to France, and Former
Secretary-General of the Western European Union,
Lecturer and Chairman of the Centre for the Study of
International Relations at the Free University of Brussels

BRASSEY'S (UK)

(A member of the Maxwell Pergamon Publishing Corporation plc)

LONDON · OXFORD · WASHINGTON · NEW YORK · BEIJING
FRANKFURT · SÃO PAULO · SYDNEY · TOKYO · TORONTO

U.K. (Editorial)	Brassey's (UK) Ltd. 24 Gray's Inn Road, London WC1X 8HR, England
(Orders)	Brassey's (UK) Ltd. Headington Hill Hall, Oxford OX3 0BW, England
U.S.A. (Editorial)	Brassey's (US) Inc., 8000 Westpark Drive, 4th Floor, McLean, Virginia 22102, U.S.A.
(Orders)	Pergamon Press, Inc., Maxwell House, Fairview Park, Elmsford, New York 10523, U.S.A.
PEOPLE'S REPUBLIC OF CHINA	Pergamon Press, Room 4037, Qianmen Hotel, Beijing, People's Republic of China
FEDERAL REPUBLIC OF GERMANY	Pergamon Press GmbH, Hammerweg 6, D-6242 Kronberg, Federal Republic of Germany
BRAZIL	Pergamon Editora Ltda, Rua Eça de Queiros, 346, CEP 04011, Paraiso, São Paulo, Brazil
AUSTRALIA	Brassey's Australia Pty. Ltd., P.O. Box 544, Potts Point, N.S.W. 2011, Australia
JAPAN	Pergamon Press, 5th Floor, Matsuoka Central Building, 1-7-1 Nishishinjuku, Shinjuku-ku, Tokyo 160, Japan
CANADA	Pergamon Press Canada Ltd., Suite No. 271, 253 College Street, Toronto, Ontario, Canada M5T 1R5

First edition 1989

Library of Congress Cataloging-in-Publication Data
Cahen, Alfred.
The Western European Union and NATO : Building a European defence identity within the context of Atlantic solidarity/Alfred Cahen. — 1st ed.
p. cm. — (Brassey's Atlantic commentaries: no 2)
1. North Atlantic Treaty Organization. 2. Western European Union. 3. Europe — Defenses. I. Title. II. Series.
UA646.3.C23 1989 355'.031'091821 — dc19 89-978

British Library Cataloguing in Publication Data
Cahen, Alfred.
The Western European Union and NATO : Building a European defence identity within the context of Atlantic solidarity. (-Brassey's Atlantic commentaries; No. 2)
1. Europe. Western Europe. Defence. Role. Western European Union.
I. Title
355'.0094

ISBN 0-08-037340-2

Printed in Great Britain by BPCC Wheatons Ltd, Exeter

Contents

CONTENTS

The Assembly and other European and Atlantic
Parliamentary Fora 34
The Assembly During the 'Somnolent' Period 34
The Role of the Assembly in the Reactivated WEU 35
The Present Role of the Assembly 35

Current Problems of the Western European Union

Current Problems of the Western
European Union 37
WEU's Reactivation: The Obstacles 37
The First Months 38
A Difficult First Task: An Approach to the
Strategic Defence Initiative 39
Current Situation 40

Current Achievements of WEU and Their
Significance for the Alliance and
Western Security 43
The Creation of a Continuous Dialogue Among Member States 43
The Emergence of Converging, or Joint, Positions 45
The Development of a European Security Identity 46
'Out-of-Area' Achievements 47

The Enlargement of the Western
European Union 51
New Members? 51
The Criteria for Possible Accession 51
The Overlapping Circles: WEU, EC, NATO 52
Portugal and Spain 53

European Co-operation in the Field of Security:
Towards a 'European Pillar' 57
Need for a European Pillar of the Alliance 57
Examples of European Co-operation in the Field of Security 59
The Impact on NATO 62
The Special Role of WEU 63

PLATE 1: Secretary-General Alfred Cahen
addressing the WEU Assembly on 5 December 1988 in Paris

PLATE 2: Sir Geoffrey Howe at the Parliamentary
Assembly of the WEU, Paris, 7 December 1988

Foreword

by
The Rt Hon Sir Geoffrey Howe, PC, QC, MP
Secretary of State for Foreign and Commonwealth Affairs

I am delighted to contribute a foreword to this survey of the WEU. I was one of the Ministers who in 1984 put in hand the revitalisation of the WEU: this document shows how much progress has since been made. I welcome it.

All the members of WEU agree that the North Atlantic Alliance needs to have a strong European pillar. At the same time, we have felt the need to develop a common defence identity as Europeans. The work on which we are embarked responds to both needs. Although the architectural and psychological metaphors may be mixed, as the quotation from David Greenwood points out elsewhere in the study, our aims are clear. Many of them were set out in the Platform on European Security Interests which we adopted last October in The Hague, and during the United Kingdom's Presidency we want to press on towards achieving them, and translating the Platform commitments into reality.

The WEU is a natural forum for discussion of key European security interests. And we should continue to seek opportunities to coordinate our policy outside Europe in the security field, as we have done so successfully in the Gulf. Last—but not least—I am delighted, as President-in-Office, that we have been able to bring discussions on enlargement with Spain and Portugal to a successful conclusion under our Presidency.

Westminster
1989

Editor's Note

The European and Atlantic political institutions which have provided the framework for the conduct of international relations between allies, partners and rivals for the past 40 years take on particular significance at a time when the pace of change in East and West is challenging assumptions and holding out prospects for a more positive international climate. Yet public opinion, which plays such a vital role in shaping the future of Europe, knows little enough about them. To many people NATO and the WEU are just names. Both alliances are dedicated to upholding the purposes and principles of the United Nations Charter. If they are to succeed in doing so they must fulfil aspirations for greater European integration without dismantling the vital transatlantic partnership which has been the cornerstone of Western security for 40 years. How this can be achieved is the central topic of this insider's view of European security concerns.

London, 1989   ERIC GROVE

Historical Background

The Birth of WEU (1948-1954)

The Brussels Treaty, in which both WEU and NATO have their origins, was conceived at the confluence of the major political currents that emerged at the end of the Second World War. On the one hand, hopes of an international world order provided by the United Nations were beginning to fade and the elements of what was to become the 'Cold War' were starting to emerge. In February 1948 the 'Prague Coup' confirmed the West's perception of the Soviet Union's expansionist and threatening ambitions, as well as the gulf that separated the East from the West. On the other hand, the building of a more united and prosperous Europe was just beginning, with the economic reconstruction stimulated by the generous and vital support of the 'Marshall Plan'.

It was against this background that France and the United Kingdom signed a Treaty of Defensive Alliance in Dunkirk on 4 March 1947. At the time, the two signatories intended the Treaty to prevent the possibility of any further military threat from Germany. But this agreement was a starting point for a wider association, since the terms of its preamble made it open to other States.

This was the situation when the United Kingdom's Foreign Secretary, Ernest Bevin, presented to the United Kingdom Cabinet, on 8 January 1948, a document entitled 'The First Aim of British Foreign Policy' which led to a speech in the House of Commons on 22 January. In those initiatives Bevin went well beyond the mere enlargement of the Dunkirk Treaty in order to include Belgium, Luxembourg and The Netherlands (Benelux). He launched the idea of an association of European nations centred around an initial nucleus formed by France, the United Kingdom and Benelux. A conference was called in Brussels on 3 March between the five nucleus states which brought about the signature of the Brussels Treaty on 17 March 1948 (for the text of that Treaty, see Appendix I).

1

The Treaty led to the establishment of an organisation known as the 'Western Union' or the 'Brussels Treaty Organisation', the forerunner of today's Western European Union. The origins and immediate purpose of the Brussels Treaty were concerned with security but the circumstances in which it was concluded, as well as its title and content, clearly indicate its role in the general process of building a united Europe. Furthermore, the signing of that diplomatic instrument was to play a major role in the launching of the Atlantic Alliance and NATO. President Truman told Congress that a great step had been taken along the road towards the building of Europe's defences, adding 'This development merits our unqualified support. I am sure that America will take the measures necessary to provide the free countries with any assistance that their situation might call for'.

On 4 April 1949, the North Atlantic Treaty was concluded in Washington. In the meantime, two things were happening on the international scene:

- progress with the building of a more united Western Europe with the establishment of the European Coal and Steel Community;
- the worsening of the 'Cold War', with the Berlin blockade and the Korean War. The confrontation between East and West reached a peak which led the West to consider the creation of a new German Army and its integration into the Atlantic Alliance. However, the fear of a resurgence of the German military tradition and memories of the First and Second World Wars remained vivid in the minds of many West European nations.

The convergence of these events was to lead to a project which was, and still is today, the most ambitious as regards European integration: the European Defence Community and its logical follow-on, the European Political Community. In 1954 both of them failed, rejected by the French National Assembly. In consequence, the question of integrating the German forces into the Atlantic command remained unresolved.

However, a solution was found by enlarging the Brussels Treaty Organisation in September 1954. This was negotiated at the London

Conference and became a reality on 23 October through the Paris Agreements which came into force on 6 May 1955. These Agreements established a Western European Union within which Germany and Italy joined the five signatories of the Brussels Treaty. They consisted of four Protocols (see Appendix I) which brought significant new features into the Treaty, the main ones being:

- wider powers of decision were foreseen for the Organisation's Permanent Council;
- each of the Member Countries undertook to restrict or give up altogether the production of certain types of weapon. The strictest restrictions were those placed on the Federal Republic of Germany. A special agency, the Agency for the Control of Armaments or ACA, was set up to supervise the application of these controls;
- a Parliamentary Assembly was established;
- the United Kingdom undertook to maintain a given number of forces on the mainland of Europe and not to withdraw them without the agreement of the majority of its partners.

These last two developments were particularly important. Democratic discussions at a European level on security matters is essential. This discussion was made possible by the establishment of the Parliamentary Assembly of Western European Union. The other development, the United Kingdom's commitment, was completely new. Never before had such an undertaking been given in peacetime *vis-à-vis* the 'Continent'.

The Paris Agreements gave Western European Union a wide area of activities. The application of the modified Treaty was entrusted to a Council endowed with powers of decision. This was a major change compared with the consultative nature of the Council of the 1948 Brussels Treaty Organisation. This Council was to be assisted by a Secretary-General and was empowered to set up any subsidiary bodies that might be necessary. The Council thereafter met at Foreign Minister and at Permanent Representative level (the London Ambassadors of the Member States and a senior official from the Foreign and Commonwealth Office). In 1955 the WEU Council set up the Standing Armaments Committee (SAC) whose purpose was to promote co-operation in military equipment production. The clear aim of the Paris Agreements was to equip the WEU with the instruments needed to develop a true

European security dimension. Whilst certainly more modest than those the European Defence Community would have covered, these instruments were nevertheless adequate and could be progressively expanded.

Under the Paris Agreements the Union was now to have two seats: London for its Permanent Council and Secretariat-General and Paris for its Parliamentary Assembly, its ACA and the International Secretariat of the SAC.

The Active Years

Between 1954 and 1973 Western European Union was to fulfil three roles of considerable importance.

1. As we have just seen, the enlargement of WEU enabled the Federal Republic of Germany to accede to the Atlantic Alliance and NATO, a major event for the two organisations.

2. In 1955 the Organisation played a fundamental role in the settlement of the Saar problem. The rich coalfields of this largely German area had been given to France in 1919 to compensate her for the losses of the First World War. The administration of the territory had been entrusted to the League of Nations, which continued to fulfil this task until the plebiscite of 1935, which returned the Saar to Germany. After the Second World War, the Saar was included in the French zone of occupation. France gave it autonomy from the Federal Republic of Germany and an economic union with France. This situation created considerable tension between the two States as well as amongst the Saarlanders. The Paris Agreements brought France and Germany to concede that a reasonable way of solving the problem might consist, first of all, in giving the Saar the opportunity of autonomy within the framework of WEU, with a referendum to determine what would finally become of the territory. This referendum was organised by WEU on 23 October 1955. The Saarlanders refused the 'Europeanisation' option by 423,000 votes to 202,000. All that remained to be done was to organise, still under the auspices of WEU, the elections which created the Landtag and marked the return of the territory to the flag of the Federal Republic.

The settlement of the Saar problem was one of the most important political achievements of WEU during the first phase of its existence; in fact, one may even go as far as to say that this problem could not have been discussed constructively except at the level of the Western European Union. It paved the way to complete Franco-German reconciliation and the development of co-operation between the two countries.

3. Between 1957, the date of the coming into force of the Treaty of Rome, which set up among six States* the European Economic Community and EURATOM, and 1973, the date of the accession of the United Kingdom to the European Communities, WEU was the only forum where the Six and the United Kingdom could meet.

However, during this first phase, Western European Union was not able—following the failure of the European Defence Community—to achieve what should have been its main objective, namely, the development of a European security dimension. Consequently, it increasingly confined itself to carrying out, under the shadow of NATO, tasks which, although not unimportant, were nevertheless increasingly routine in nature.

The Somnolent Years (1973-1984)

When the United Kingdom did accede to the European Communities, WEU lost its remaining role and slipped into a kind of lethargy. Between 1973 and 1984 there were no meetings at ministerial level. Its only vital element was the Parliamentary Assembly which continued to call for the creation of a European security dimension and the reactivation of the Organisation. However, as there was no 'executive' to which these calls could be addressed, the voice of the Parliamentary Assembly remained unheard.

The Reactivation (1984-?)

Why, in 1983 and early 1984, did the WEU member states decide to arouse the Organisation and 'reactivate' it? The answer to this question

* Belgium, France, Federal Republic of Germany, Italy, Luxembourg, the Netherlands.

would seem to be found in the dual context in which the Organisation has existed from the start—namely, the process of building Europe and the maintenance of Atlantic solidarity.

At the beginning of the 1980s, two important trends were making an impact on the European scene:

1. Both governments and public opinion were beginning to show a marked interest in European security for the following reasons:

- as 'détente' was giving way to a return to the 'Cold War', certain differences of opinion were emerging between Washington and its European allies about their perception of common security. Whilst there was determination not to jeopardise Atlantic solidarity, Europe was seeking to have a greater say within the Alliance and have more influence in the management of East-West relations;
- at a time when the European Communities were facing grave problems and going from one crisis to another, there was increasing temptation to look elsewhere for progress in the building of Europe which was lacking in the context of the Communities;
- further, there was a noticeable increase of interest shown, both by European public opinion and governments, in problems relating to the defence of Europe. There was increasing discussion of defence in the media, in specialised research centres, in administrations and political parties. The deployment of INF nuclear missiles on the territory of five States of Western Europe led an increasing section of European public opinion to question the Atlantic dimension of European security. It was becoming increasingly obvious to these governments of Western Europe that were members of the Atlantic Alliance that a large section of their peoples no longer considered the notion of security as something affecting them personally but something distant, 'manipulated' from outside in another country. It was thus becoming a matter of urgency to bring the peoples of Western Europe closer to a notion of their own security—in the context of common Atlantic security.

2. Despite the creation of 'European Political Co-operation', the inability of the European Communities, (the 'Ten', later the 'Twelve') to provide a security dimension to European unity had become increasingly clear to all. This was essentially because of the reservations in this matter by three of the countries, Denmark, Greece and Ireland. Another way thus had to be found to achieve this European security dimension.

French interest in Europe's security problems had been evident for some time. It was therefore not surprising that Paris—in the person of the Minister for Foreign Affairs, Mr. Claude Cheysson—should have taken the initiative at the beginning of February 1984, by circulating to the Member States a memorandum containing a number of proposals regarding the reactivation of WEU. The idea was that some genuine tasks should be restored to the Organisation and that its rules and institutions should be adapted to the new circumstances and to the responsibilities proposed for it.

Coincidentally, an article by the Belgian Foreign Minister, Mr. Tindemans, published in *Le Monde* on 23 December of the previous year, mooted a number of ideas very clearly anticipating the French document. Having already secured the support of the Federal Republic of Germany, the French Government then contacted the Belgian Government, in January 1984, for its backing, before publishing its document; the document immediately received the approval of Brussels in the form of a paper complementing the one issued by France.

From that time on, events were to move fairly quickly and the reactivation of WEU was agreed upon and set in train in three successive stages:

- a meeting of the Foreign Ministers in Paris, on 12 June 1984;
- a meeting of the Foreign and Defence Ministers in Rome, on 26-27 October 1984;
- a meeting of the Foreign and Defence Ministers in Bonn, on 22-23 April 1985.

It was the Rome meeting which adopted the Declaration which, in a way, was the 'certificate of rebirth' for Western European Union (see Appendix II). In this document the 'Seven' defined the roles that they intended to give to the reactivated Organisation and the commitments that they were undertaking to ensure that this reactivation became a reality. Effective implementation of reactivation developed from the meeting in Bonn. In the following chapters we shall see what successes it has achieved and also what problems it encountered.

The Reactivated Western European Union as Part of the Process of European Construction

Developing a European Security Dimension

The problem of creating a European security dimension has existed since the countries of Western Europe—or at least some of them—began their process of co-operation and integration. As that seasoned trade unionist, Ernest Bevin, then British Foreign Secretary, put it to the House of Commons on 22 January 1948, after spelling out the increasingly menacing signs of Soviet expansionism,

> 'Surely, these developments point to the conclusion that the free nations of Western Europe must now draw closer together. How much these countries have in common! Our sacrifices in the war, our hatred of injustice and oppression, our parliamentary democracies, our striving for economic rights, our love of liberty. I believe the time is ripe for the consolidation of Western Europe'.

When Bevin spoke of 'Western Europe', he was thinking primarily of his own country, France, the Benelux and also Italy. Some three years after the end of World War II, he also included Germany 'but only when it has become a democracy'.

This London initiative led, on 17 March 1948, to the signing of the Brussels Treaty. The Act created an Alliance, between the five signatory Parties (Belgium, France, Luxembourg, the Netherlands, the United Kingdom) which formally committed each of the participating States to the defence of any one of them, should it be the victim of an act of aggression. But, what was more, this Brussels Treaty marked an important stage in the process of European construction. One has only to read the text of the document to realise this. Indeed, the very title of the Pact and its preamble are clear in this regard. The document is called 'Treaty of Economic, Social and Cultural Collaboration and Collective Self Defence'. Its preamble clearly commits the signatories to strengthen general European ties (see Appendix I—opening five paragraphs).

This European dimension was to be further reaffirmed and strengthened a few years later, when the Treaty of Brussels was modified by the Paris Agreements enlarging the Pact to the Federal Republic of Germany and Italy. In these agreements the signatories added a new paragraph to the Preamble committing themselves 'to promote the unity and to encourage the progressive integration of Europe'.

It is worth noting, furthermore, that the Brussels Treaty came into being against the general background of growing moves towards European co-operation and integration. It was practically contemporaneous with the Treaty setting up the Organisation for European Economic Co-operation, or OEEC, in Paris on 16 April 1948. It was also almost contemporaneous with the Agreement creating the Council of Europe in London on 5 May 1949. It was only three years older than the Act establishing the European Coal and Steel Community, or ECSC, signed in Paris on 8 April 1951 as the first step towards what was to become the Europe of the Six, then the Nine and Ten and now the Twelve.

There then ensued the abortive attempt to combine the security dimension contained in the Brussels Treaty with the supranational character of the ECSC, in that most ambitious project in the process of building Europe, the European Defence Community (EDC).

The idea of the realisation of a European Defence Community carried with it, as a logical consequence, an attempt to create a European Political Community with competences in the field of economics, foreign relations and security policies. It would have a supranational character, with a two-headed Executive (a Council of Ministers from each Member State and an appointed 'Executive Council'), a bi-cameral Assembly (a House directly elected and a Senate made up of members designated by the national parliaments), and a President of the Executive Council, appointed by the Senate, who was to be responsible to the House.

It is clear that if the European Defence Community (and the European

Political Community) had been approved in the first half of the 1950s, the European Union—which the governments of the Twelve are now seeking, especially since the European Summit of The Hague in 1969—would virtually have been achieved more than 30 years ago. However, EDC failed in 1954 when, after the British had refused to join, the French Assembly voted to 'pass on to other business' rather than approve it.

The Continuing Efforts to Develop a European Security Dimension

The crisis caused by the failure of EDC led to the Paris Agreements of October 1954, enlarging the Treaty of Brussels to the Federal Republic of Germany and Italy, and transforming the Brussels Treaty Organisation into a Western European Union. In that first phase of its existence, however, that is from 1954 to 1983, WEU did not prove itself capable of fulfilling the task of developing a European security dimension.

Efforts were, therefore, undertaken in other frameworks to achieve this goal. One could even say that in the graveyard of aborted attempts to bring about a European Union, a graveyard where the tombs are many, the most numerous ones contain the remains of the initiatives devoted to the creation of a European security dimension.

There were the two 'Plans Fouchet' in the 1960s, followed by the document on a European identity published in Copenhagen on 14 December 1973 by the Foreign Ministers of what were still the Nine stressing that foreign policy and security aspects had an important role in the achievement of a more united Europe. Then there came the famous 'Tindemans Report', completed in December 1975, at the request of the member countries of the Communities (meeting as the European Council in Paris in December 1974)—and just as valid and topical now as it was then—declaring that European Union will not be complete until it has a common defence policy. For their part, both the European Parliament and the Assembly of Western European Union have committed themselves to work towards the establishment of such a policy. On 14 February 1984 the European Parliament approved the Draft Treaty establishing European Union. This clearly includes security questions within the proposed Union's competences. In the first article of title III 'Principles and Methods of Action' paragraph 1 states that:

> 'The Union shall direct its efforts in international relations towards the achievement of peace through the peaceful settlement of conflict and towards security, the deterrence of aggression, détente, the mutual balance and verifiable reduction of military forces and armaments, respect for human rights, the raising of living standards in the Third World, the expansion and improvement of international economic and monetary relations in general and trade in particular and the strengthening of international organisation'.

The Assembly of Western European Union has not only been the melting pot for excellent and substantial reports on this subject, it also served as a platform in 1982—with the same aim in view—for the French Defence Minister, M. Charles Hernu.

Furthermore, spurred on by the European Parliament, the Commission of the European Communities, acting on the impetus given by, amongst others, its Vice-President, Commissioner Etienne Davignon, set about the task of bringing the production of military equipment (and especially conventional weapons) within the ambit of the Communities' industrial policy. All this effort was to little avail.

There did, however, seem to be an institution whose vocation seemed to be the centre for developing a European security dimension and that was the European Political Co-operation of the Six, then of the Nine, then of the Ten and today of the Twelve. European Political Co-operation is an effort to harmonize the foreign policies of the Member States. It is difficult to discuss foreign policy without including security matters.

So it was in the framework of European Political Co-operation that the efforts to develop a European security dimension were pursued the most vigorously in the 1980s. There was first the initiative of the British presidency in the second half of 1981 to give competence in the field of security to European Political Co-operation. This initiative led to six months of very tough and difficult negotiations. When those negotiations were completed and the London Report adopted in December 1981, the result was a half success or, rather, a half failure. Political Co-operation did not receive competence to deal with security problems as such but only with the political aspects of security.

The effort was almost immediately resumed under the aegis of two great European Statesmen: Mr. Colombo, then Minister of Foreign Affairs of Italy, and Mr. Genscher, Minister of Foreign Affairs of the Federal Republic of Germany. They produced the 'Genscher-Colombo Initiative'. This time, the negotiations—equally tough and difficult— lasted some eighteen months. They were concluded in June 1983 by the Solemn Declaration of Stuttgart which indeed is an important step in the direction of the creation of a European Union. But, in the field of security, the result was once again a half failure. The Twelve did not receive competence to deal with the security problems as such, but only with the political and economic aspects of security.

The Single European Act of December 1985 did not go much beyond that. Certainly, it recognises, in its article 30(6), the principle that

> 'the High Contracting Parties consider that closer co-operation on questions of European security would contribute in an essential way to the development of a European identity in external policy matters'.

But the same article 30(6) adds immediately that

> 'they are ready to coordinate their positions more closely on the political and economic aspects of security'.

The same article notes that

> 'nothing in this Title shall impede closer co-operation in the field of security between certain of the High Contracting Parties within the framework of the Western European Union or the Atlantic Alliance'.

But that last part was not adopted without great difficulty.

Why all these partial successes, or rather, half failures? Because three of what were then the Ten—today the Twelve—were not able to accept a European security dimension as such. They were: Ireland, Denmark and Greece. And so, the other Seven turned once more to the 'old WEU' to try and reactivate it as the possible start of a European security dimension.

Western European Union, the Communities and European Political Co-operation

The Western European Union is an element of the European construction: not at the same level as the European Communities or European Political Co-operation—because there are only seven (soon to be nine) members and not twelve—but certainly at their side. This has important consequences:

- one of them is that WEU has to keep a very close contact with the other elements of the construction of Europe;
- the second is that a change in the membership of the European Communities and European Political Co-operation has necessarily some consequence for Western European Union. The best proof of that is that, even before signing their treaty of accession to the European Communities and to European Political Co-operation, Portugal and Spain made their interest to join WEU known very clear, and that Turkey, at the same time as it applied for full membership of the European Communities and to Political Co-operation, indicated it was interested in joining Western European Union;
- and of course, in the third place, any major change of substance in the evolution of the European construction of the Twelve must necessarily have importance for Western European Union. Because, after all, if everyone among the Twelve* was able to accept, truly and without afterthoughts, a full European security dimension, the WEU should put its future and even its very existence into question, and be ready to melt in the mainstream of the construction of Europe. But as long as that is not the case, Western European Union is the only place where its Member States can reflect together and act in concert about their security problems.

The centre of the process of constructing Europe is, however, without any doubt, constituted by what is called the 'Europe of the Twelve'. This Europe has an economic dimension with the European

---

* Belgium, Denmark, Federal Republic of Germany, France, Greece, Ireland, Italy, Luxembourg, the Netherlands, Portugal, Spain, the United Kingdom.

Communities (Coal and Steel Community, European Economic Community, Euratom). It has, with European Political Co-operation, a foreign policy dimension. But it has no security dimension, and it is WEU which, at this stage, plays that role. Political Co-operation, as well as WEU, is only intergovernmental in nature. In this regard, the supranational Communities must remain the legitimate foundation for constructing a united Europe.

Moreover, the Communities were given by their founding fathers the prospects of developing into a European Union, with not only economic competence but also powers in the field of foreign policy and security. The hope of such an achievement was almost fulfilled, with the Draft Treaty regarding the establishment of a European Political Community which appeared as the logical consequence of the European Defence Community. Since then, progress in that direction has been extremely slow and, in some respects, non-existent but this has not prevented the Communities from remaining faithful to this goal.

It is against this background that the initiatives taken in the field of European security by the President of the Commission of the European Communities, M. Jacques Delors, must be seen. It was in mid-March 1987 that he put forward a proposal to convene a meeting of the European Council (Heads of States and Governments) whose purpose would have been not only to adopt a European position on the then current disarmament negotiations, but also to 'lay the foundations for a European security policy'.

He knew that this initiative stood very little chance of being accepted by the whole of the Twelve, and that it would meet with the opposition of at least Ireland, Denmark, and possibly Greece. This is indeed what happened. But he thought, and rightly so, that it was his duty to stand up in this respect and remind European public opinion of the real destiny of the Communities.

He later expressed his views to some journalists in The Hague on 12 July 1987, when answering the question 'Can defence be the driving force for the revival of Europe?' He recalled in that connection that, in the view of the founding fathers of Europe, the purpose of European integration was to ensure peace among its citizens but that, even at that time, peace carried with it the idea of defence, as evidenced by the proposals for Political Union in 1952 and for a European Defence

Community (EDC). He added that Europeans 'should equip themselves with a defence institution in the wider conventional field including theatre weapons which belong to them', that this was possible only 'if there was a single Community' and

> 'a political institution which would group together all those members of the Community who wished to be associated with it and which, for the time being, would be separate from the Economic Community (...) and this political institution should concern itself either with defence only or with defence and foreign policy (...) As in the field of economic affairs, the steering body would be the meeting of Heads of Government'.

In the same perspective, he was to say somewhat later, in a speech he delivered in September 1987 on the occasion of the opening of the academic year of the '*Institut Royal Supérieur de Défense*' of Belgium:

> 'As regards institutions, my hope lies in the reactivation of WEU and its ability to play in the future the necessary role as an interface between the European Community, Political Co-operation and the Atlantic Alliance. This hope is based on the fact that since its reactivation which it must be stressed, has occurred in a somewhat less than favourable context—reply to the unilateral announcement of the SDI programme, the Reykjavik meeting, the speeding-up of the Geneva talks—it has been possible, through WEU and the frequent and regular meeting of Defence and Foreign Affairs Ministers of its seven Member States, to begin in-depth reflection on Europe's defence'.

It is not surprising, in these circumstances, that the Secretariat-General of WEU has a very close contact with the Communities and that the Secretary-General remains in close relation both with President Delors—regarding the overall policies developing in the context of the edification of a European Union—and with the Vice-President of the Commission, in charge of the industrial questions, Mr. Narjes, regarding a possible European organised market for military equipment. All this must be seen in the perspective of the creation of a single European market foreseen for 1992 with all the political consequences thereof.

It is in the European Political Co-operation of the Twelve, and not in a reactivated WEU, that a European security dimension should have developed. But, as far as European Political Co-operation (EPC) and security problems are concerned, from the very beginning there has been an ambiguity that, in spite of all efforts, it has still not been possible to remove.

From its beginning, EPC had to deal with an issue whose security aspect is clearly of great importance, the Conference on Security and Co-operation in Europe (CSCE). Indeed, one of the main items on the agenda of its first ministerial meeting in Munich in November 1970 was precisely this issue.

Furthermore, not only has this subject been kept on its agenda, but the 'security' dimension—with the Conference on Confidence and Security Building Measures and Disarmament in Europe (CDE)—has come increasingly to the forefront. Indeed, concentration on the CSCE has been a major success for Political Co-operation and played a particularly positive role in its development.

The question may be asked why EPC, which remains so timid with respect to security, has been so successful in an area where not only are such problems present but where their importance is increasing. The answer is probably that the CSCE does not deal exclusively with them and, in addition, they were less important at the outset than at present. Also not recognising the importance of East-West relations—and this is what would have happened if EPC had ignored the Conference on Security and Co-operation in Europe in all its aspects—would have denied EPC any importance from its very beginning. In the event, the CSCE has had a very positive effect on the development of EPC.

For many problems, however, the areas of responsibility of the two bodies are very close. For example, let us take the situation in the Gulf. European Political Co-operation deals with the issue from the foreign policy angle, whereas WEU deals with it from the security angle. Here, too, concerted action between the two fora is essential. At the present time, however, this is only achieved at the level of liaison between the two Secretariat Heads.

WEU and Atlantic Solidarity

WEU and NATO: An Intimate Relationship

The Atlantic Alliance and WEU have been closely linked from the very beginning. Both the Brussels Treaty—signed on 17 March 1948—which forms the basis of WEU, and the Washington Treaty which established the Atlantic Alliance on 4 April 1949, stem from a similar international context, identical preoccupations, the same determination and ideals. The States of Western Europe and of North America needed to take urgent steps to counter an ever-increasing threat and to be able to defend their democratic freedom.

It may indeed be said that the Brussels Treaty led directly to the Washington Treaty. The adoption by the five European States of the Brussels Treaty was one of the main arguments used by President Truman to obtain the US Senate's approval of the Washington Treaty. It was no coincidence that the American President's speech, which launched the idea of the Atlantic Alliance, was made on the very same day that the Belgian, French, Luxembourg, Netherlands and United Kingdom Ministers were in Belgium to sign the Brussels Treaty.

The evolution of the Alliance and NATO and that of WEU was not the same, but the institutions remained closely linked. Only one example is needed to illustrate this fact. When the failure of the EDC in 1954 made it impossible to use this avenue to allow the Federal Republic of Germany to accede to the Atlantic Alliance and NATO, it was through the enlargement of WEU to include the Federal Republic (and Italy) that this event, essential to the Alliance, could take place. Moreover, on the occasion of this enlargement, a new Article IV was added to the Brussels Treaty formalising relations between NATO and WEU (see Appendix I, pp. 71 and 76).

The Reactivation of WEU and Atlantic Solidarity

In the various negotiations leading to the reactivation of the Organisation, its relations with the Alliance were spelt out very clearly. They demonstrated, in fact, that each of the seven member States of WEU considered that there was no credible defence of the West—and thus Western Europe—without the Atlantic Alliance. Hence, the reactivation of WEU took place not outside, but in the very context of the Alliance. This is amply proved by the Rome Declaration, whose Paragraphs 4, 5 and 6 are quite unequivocal in the matter (see Appendix II).

The fact that the reactivation of the Organisation took place within the Alliance has, of course, important consequences. One of them is that WEU must keep the closest contact with the Atlantic Alliance. This is achieved by regular exchanges of information between the Presidency of the WEU and the North Atlantic Council. There is also an ongoing relationship between the two Secretaries-General and their staffs.

The 'Platform on European Security Interests'

The 'Platform on European Security Interests' adopted by the WEU Ministers in The Hague on 27 October 1987, which is a first definition of a European security identity placed in the context of Atlantic solidarity, could not be more explicit (see Section I,4 of Appendix III).

This 'Platform' (which is reproduced in full as Appendix III) is constructed around three main sets of ideas:

- the conditions of European security;
- the criteria on which European security is based;
- the responsibilities of Europeans with regard to their security considered in the context of common Atlantic security, whether in the areas of defence, arms control or dialogue with the East.

In the context of Atlantic solidarity it represents major committments by the seven Member States of WEU. The two main ones are contained in Paragraphs 3 and 4 of Section III (see Appendix III, pp. 94-5).

The previous American Administration fully acknowledged the

importance of this document for Atlantic solidarity: it is sufficient to quote the speech made on 4 November 1987 by President Reagan:

'(...) Last week, the Foreign and Defence Ministers of the Western European Union issued an impressive declaration. It reaffirmed the importance of maintaining our nuclear and conventional deterrents and affirmed a positive Western European identity in the field of defence within the framework of the Atlantic Alliance. We welcome these developments'.

Furthermore, this 'Platform' played a significant and positive role at the Atlantic Summit on 2 and 3 March 1988. The spirit and substance of a number of its passages were effectively reproduced in the latter's Final Communiqué. This is clear from a comparison between the text of the 'Platform' and that of the Communiqué.
Let us proceed to this comparison:

TABLE 1: *How the Platform on European Security Interests is Reflected in the Final Communiqué of the Atlantic Summit 2-3 March 1988*

PLATFORM ON EUROPEAN SECURITY INTERESTS	ATLANTIC SUMMIT— FINAL COMMUNIQUÉ
I.1* Europe remains at the centre of East-West relations and, forty years after the end of the Second World War, a divided continent. The human consequences of this division remain unacceptable, although certain concrete improvements have been made on a bilateral level and on the basis of the Helsinki Final Act. We owe it to our people to overcome this situation and to exploit in the interest of all Europeans the opportunities for further improvements which may present themselves.	7-2** We want gradually to overcome the unnatural division of the European continent, which affects most directly the German people. We will continue to uphold the freedom and viability of Berlin and to support efforts to improve the situation there.
I.3 We have not yet witnessed any lessening of the military build-up which the Soviet Union has sustained over so many years. The geostrategic situation of Western Europe makes it particularly vulnerable to the superior conventional, chemical and nuclear forces of the Warsaw Pact. This is the fundamental problem for European security. The	9. However, we have to date witnessed no relaxation of the military effort pursued for years by the Soviet Union. The Soviet Union persists in deploying far greater military forces than are required for its defence. This massive force, which the Soviet Union has not refrained from using outside its borders, as is still the case in Afghanistan, constitutes a

Warsaw Pact's superior conventional forces and its capability for surprise attack and large-scale offensive action are of special concern in this context.

fundamental source of tension between East and West. The steady growth of Soviet military capabilities, as it affects every region of the Alliance, requires our constant attention.

I.4 Under these conditions the security of the Western European countries can only be ensured in close association with our North American allies. The security of the Alliance is indivisible. The partnership between the two sides of the Atlantic rests on the twin foundations of shared values and interests. Just as the commitment of the North American democracies is vital to Europe's security, a free, independent and increasingly more united Western Europe is vital to the security of North America.

4-2,3 Likewise, a free, independent and increasingly united Europe is vital to North America's security. The credibility of Allied defence cannot be maintained without a major European contribution. We therefore welcome recent efforts to reinforce the European pillar of the Alliance, intended to strengthen the transatlantic partnership, and Alliance security as a whole.

The Atlantic Alliance cannot be strong if Europe is weak.

I.5 It is our conviction that the balanced policy of the Harmel Report remains valid. Political solidarity and adequate military strength within the Atlantic Alliance, arms control, disarmament and the search for genuine détente continue to be integral parts of this policy. Military security and a policy of détente are not contradictory but complementary.

3. Our concept of a balanced security policy as set out in the Harmel Report has successfully stood the test of time. It remains valid in its two complementary and mutually reinforcing approaches: political solidarity and adequate military strength, and, on that basis, the search for constructive dialogue and co-operation, including arms control. The ultimate political purpose of our Alliance is to achieve a just and lasting peaceful order in Europe.

II. 2 In the present circumstances and as far as we can foresee, there is no alternative to the Western strategy for the prevention of war, which has ensured peace in freedom for an unprecedented period of European history. To be credible and effective, the strategy of deterrence and defence must continue to be based on an adequate mix of appropriate nuclear and conventional forces, only the nuclear element of which can confront a potential aggressor with an unacceptable risk.

5. Our aim will continue to be to prevent any kind of war or intimidation. By maintaining credible deterrence the Alliance has secured peace in Europe for nearly forty years. Conventional defences alone cannot ensure this; therefore, for the foreseeable future there is no alternative to the Alliance strategy for the prevention of war. This is a strategy of deterrence based upon appropriate mix of adequate and effective nuclear and conventional forces which will continue to be kept up to date where necessary.

II.3 The substantial presence of US conventional and nuclear forces plays an irreplaceable part in the defence of Europe. They embody the American commitment to the defence of Europe and provide the indispensable linkage with the US strategic deterrent.

4. The security in freedom and the prosperity of the European and North American Allies are inextricably linked. The long-standing commitment of the North American democracies to the preservation of peace and security in Europe is vital. The presence in Europe of the conventional and nuclear forces of the United States provides the essential linkage with the United States strategic deterrent, and, together with the forces of Canada, is a tangible expression of that commitment. This presence must and will be maintained.

II.5 Arms control and disarmament are an integral part of Western security policy and not an alternative to it. They should lead to a stable balance of forces at the lowest level compatible with our security. Arms control policy should, like our defence policy, take into account the specific European security interests in an evolving situation. It must be consistent with the maintenance of the strategic unity of the Alliance and should not preclude closer European defence cooperation. Arms control agreements have to be effectively verifiable and stand the test of time. East and West have a common interest in achieving this.

11. Arms control is an integral part of our security policy. We seek negotiations not for their own sake but to reach agreements which can significantly reduce the risk of conflict and make a genuine contribution to stability and peace. We shall work together vigorously and on the basis of the closest consultation to this end.

III.c.1 The common responsibility of all Europeans is not only to preserve the peace but to shape it constructively. The Helsinki Final Act continues to serve as our guide to the fulfilment of the objective of gradually overcoming the division of Europe. We shall therefore continue to make full use of the CSCE process in order to promote comprehensive cooperation among all participating States.

III.c.2 The possibilities contained in the Final Act should be fully exploited. We therefore intend:
—to seek to increase the transparency of

16. The resolution of East-West differences will require progress in many fields. Genuine peace in Europe cannot be established solely by arms control. It must be firmly based on full respect for fundamental human rights. As we continue our efforts to reduce armaments, we shall press for implementation on the part of the governments of the Soviet Union and of other Eastern countries of all of the principles and provisions of the Helsinki Final Act and of the Madrid Concluding Document. We support the continuation and strengthening of the CSCE process. It represents an important

military potential and activities and the calculability of behaviour in accordance with the Stockholm Document of 1986 by further confidence-building measures.
—vigorously to pursue our efforts to provide for the full respect of human rights without which no genuine peace is possible.
—to open new mutually beneficial possibilities in the fields of economy, technology, science and the protection of the environment.
—to achieve more opportunities for the people in the whole of Europe to move freely and to exchange opinions and information and to intensify cultural exchanges, and thus to promote concrete improvements for the benefit of all people in Europe.

means of promoting stable and constructive relations on a long term basis between countries of East and West, and, moreover, enhances closer and more fruitful contacts between peoples and individuals throughout Europe. We call upon all participating States to make every effort for an early conclusion to the CSCE follow-up meeting in Vienna with a substantial and balanced final document.

NOTES
  * Section reference
  ** Paragraph reference

WEU and 'Burden-sharing'

In the context of transatlantic relations the old problem of 'burden-sharing' has perhaps taken on greater importance today than ever before. This question has made regular appearances on the Alliance's agenda over the past three decades. The issue in this matter is to define how the resource burden of the Alliance's security arrangements should be calculated and fairly distributed among allies.

'Burden-sharing' has normally been put on the agenda by the United States in the belief that they are carrying a disproportionate share of the load. In the early years of the Atlantic partnership, the United States accepted that it should shoulder the major part of the burden of Western security to the benefit of an exhausted Western Europe. The Americans also hoped to reconstruct and transform Europe into a sound and secure entity through the extensive economic assistance provided under the Marshall Plan. However, as soon as Europe became more prosperous, America started to become increasingly critical of those allied countries whose economic growth did not seem to them to be accompanied by a commensurate increase in the resources the European nations allocated to defence. In these circumstances, the accusations of European 'free-riding' at American expense started to multiply. Furthermore, this American feeling has increased as Europe—organising itself in the framework of the European Economic Community—started to emerge, in the eyes of its American allies, as an economic competitor, not to say an unfair one. The belief that this European competition is due—at least partly—to the savings Western Europe countries are making in their defence budgets, allowing them to use the money for other purposes so that, effectively, this European competition is, in the end, being financed by the American tax-payer, did not take long to surface. Hence, the problem of burden-sharing became a fact of the Alliance's life over the years and one that remains with us today. It has had its moments of great acuteness and others when it has acquired a somewhat ritualistic character, but it has been there since as early as the beginning of the 1950s and its importance has steadily increased.

However, the problem has never seemed as predominant as it does today. The debate is an important one, first in itself, and second because of the impact it is bound to have on the future of the Atlantic Alliance and on the links existing between the North American allies and the European ones. It would be wrong and potentially disastrous, at this stage, for the Europeans to try and duck it.

I am glad to say that that is not their intention. As a recent Secretary-General of the Western European Union, I can speak in this respect, for that Organisation's Member States with no hesitation whatsoever. At the same time, we must all be aware that if the matter is not addressed in a serious and statesmanlike manner and in a spirit of true Atlantic solidarity, it could become extremely dangerous for the West.

Why? First of all because that debate—from the start, and more and more since—has often been characterised more by passion and demagogy than by the rational thinking which should prevail in such an important matter. An indication of this reality is that the conclusions of some thoroughly researched Pentagon reports on the subject are—as soon as they imply that the European allies are contributing in an important share (not to say a fair one) to the common defence—totally ignored by important sectors of US public opinion and, even more important, sectors of Congressional opinion. On the other side of the ocean, evidence of this can be found in the reactions of those for whom the question of burden-sharing is not the subject of a cool assessment of the various aspects of the problem as such, but rather the occasion of accusations against either 'the US hegemonic arrogance' or 'the US return to isolationism', if not both at the same time. From this it is—so it seems to me—evident that such attitudes convey instinctive and subjective reactions rather than a rational and balanced approach to the situation.

Secondly, the burden-sharing debate has been too often a surrogate for much more difficult arguments like American doubts about its European allies' determination or even loyalty and European doubts about the wisdom of some American policies or the strength of the United States' nuclear umbrella.

Thirdly, such an approach is encouraged by the fact that it is rather difficult to tackle the problem of burden-sharing with mere figures. No matter how comprehensive the analysis, comparisons that depend on selected economic data or static force levels can describe no more than a portion of the real picture, as Assistant Secretary of State, Rosanne Ridgeway, very rightly pointed out in her testimony before the Congressional panel on burden-sharing (15 March 1988). However, the temptation is always great—all the more so as it provides an easy solution—to turn to overall figures (percentage of GNP, of GNP per capita, or of the national budgets devoted to defence expenditure) and to draw from them definite conclusions.

So, if this problem is badly managed it could have regrettable or even disastrous consequences for Atlantic solidarity. It is vital then that it should be approached in a positive spirit of solidarity and considered as a problem that is common to all the allies. This is what WEU, for its part, is attempting to do.

Evidence of it appears in WEU's 'Platform' where it is stated that its Member States will 'see to it that the level of each country's contribution to the common defence adequately reflects its capabilities'. Again, there is evidence in the fact that for the first time—under a sort of 'WEU umbrella'—five of its members are working side by side with the American forces in a region outside the immediate zone of European security and Atlantic defence, namely, the Gulf. This constitutes, in a certain way, an 'out-of-area' Euro-American 'burden-sharing' which constitutes a novelty. We will see later its exact substance and scope. Finally, consultations among the countries of Western Europe have started and are continuing on the allocation and management of defence resources so as to improve efficiency. This should enable the seven WEU Member States to shoulder their share in the common Atlantic defence.

Thus, WEU is endeavouring to create the conditions for a discussion which is not divisive for the Alliance but is fruitful and likely to strengthen it.

WEU, an Element for Strengthening the Atlantic Alliance

Legally, the Brussels Treaty is a very binding form of alliance. Hence, at the very beginning, the Organisation had the defence structures necessary for carrying out its mission. However, with the signing of the Washington Treaty, its implementation and the subsequent establishment of NATO, the Organisation gave up these defence structures and transferred its military activities to the North Atlantic Treaty Organisation. No clearer proof could have been given of the commitment to Atlantic solidarity of its Member States, or of the fact that they believed that their defence lay within the Alliance, or of their readiness to act accordingly.

When the Member States of WEU decided to reactivate the Organisation, certain fears were nevertheless expressed by those allies that were not members of it about the creation of an element of division within the Alliance. Indeed, when, at the very beginning of the WEU reactivation in the first half of 1985, it was decided to convene a meeting of high-ranking experts in the field of arms control under the Organisation's aegis, the State Department—and in the person of its Assistant Secretary for European affairs Mr. (now Ambassador) Richard Burt—expressed to the seven Member States the concern of the United States that such an initiative could lead to different—if not diverging—positions in the Alliance regarding arms control negotiations. It took some time after that for the State Department to look upon WEU with less concern and finally with a positive confidence.

In reality, WEU has spared no effort to avoid any such division. On the contrary, it has proved itself to be a strengthening factor for the Alliance. In this respect, WEU has successfully subjected its action to three requirements that I personally discussed with NATO leaders, in particular the former Secretary-General, Lord Carrington, who defined them as follows:

- the actions of WEU must be compatible with the objectives of the activities of the Alliance;
- they must be transparent for those allies which are not members of WEU and who must be sufficiently informed about what is going on in order not to feel excluded;
- they must aim to increase the 'Seven's' commitment towards Atlantic solidarity.

The Role of the Reactivated Western European Union

A Firm and Binding Alliance

The reactivation of Western European Union leaves intact the substance of the Brussels Treaty, as modified by the Paris Agreements. Article V states that

> 'if any of the High Contracting parties should be the object of an armed attack in Europe, the other High Contracting Parties will, in accordance with the provisions of Article 51 of the Charter of the United Nations, afford the Party so attacked all the military and other aid and assistance in their power'.

Theoretically, this Article goes further than Article 5 of the Washington Treaty which does not provide for the same automatic intervention by the allies. The difference, however, is eroded by the fact that within NATO there is an integrated military command which leads to the same result.

New Responsibilities

The Rome Declaration—adopted on 27 October 1984 and which is the 'Act of Rebirth' of the Organisation—does however add to WEU a new and important responsibility by making WEU the European centre for the Member States' common reflection and concerted action on security matters (see Appendix II).

WEU must, therefore, assert itself as a forum for European political co-operation on security. Its objectives will be to establish among its member countries an ongoing dialogue and to reach a convergence of views or even common positions and thus some kind of European security identity in the framework, of course, of Atlantic solidarity. In this context, the Rome Declaration provides that the Member States will hold 'comprehensive discussions and seek to harmonise their views on the specific conditions of security in Europe' (see paragraph 8 of Appendix II).

All this means that—in the field of defence, arms control and the consequences of the development of East-West relations for Europe's security—the Organisation must strive to achieve convergent and, if possible, common positions on all issues which are, in this respect, of topical relevance for its members. It must do so, however, in a spirit of Atlantic solidarity in order to avoid creating any risk of Alliance division; indeed, it must do so in such a way as to strengthen the Alliance.

This is a duty which WEU has set itself since the beginning of re-activation even though initially it meant adopting a 'low profile' so as not to appear as an 'exclusive club' within the framework of Atlantic solidarity. Generally, the Organisation—with this aim in view—abstained from adopting publicly, between 1985 and 1986, positions as such. It only began to adopt such positions when it became clear to all that its action was well and truly in the context of, and offered a contribution to, Atlantic solidarity. The 'Platform on European Security Interests', which its Ministers adopted on 27 October 1987, was recognised as a 'plus' for the West as a whole.

Secondly, it means that WEU has a role to play with regard to European armaments co-operation. This subject has long occupied the attention of both the European allies and the Alliance in general. In 1955, it was decided to give WEU responsibility in this field and to set up under its auspices a 'Standing Armaments Committee' made up of representatives of the Defence Ministries of the Member States and assisted by an International Secretariat. This was quite logical since, at that time, there was no other body in Western Europe charged with this essential task. This Standing Armaments Committee played an active role in the following years, even during the somnolent period in the Organisation's history.

In the meantime, however, efforts have been made in the same direction in much wider fora, in particular:

- in the Independent European Programme Group, which comprises thirteen countries, i.e. virtually all the European members of NATO*;
- in the European Communities and, more particularly, the Economic Community.

As is known, the IEPG approaches the problem of European arms cooperation on a 'project-by-project' basis, whereas the Community puts it in the perspective of its general industrial policies and the possible organisation of a market capable of bringing about a rationalisation in the field of arms procurement.

In my opinion, these two contexts are not contradictory but complementary. In this connection, it is important that WEU does not hinder either the work of the IEPG or that of the European Communities§. It must ensure that its members provide, in a concerted manner, the political impetus needed to promote positive results within the IEPG on the one hand, and the Communities on the other. This task is made easier for them in that they are like-minded from the point of view of their strategic options—even though France is not a member of the integrated military structure of NATO—and are homogeneous from an industrial point of view.

Lastly, reactivating WEU means that there is the role of the Organisation *vis-à-vis* crises occurring in regions not directly linked to the European security zone or to the zone of Atlantic solidarity. The question of possible allied action outside the specific area of Atlantic solidarity has been a matter of controversy within the Alliance. Whenever it has arisen, it has led to an academic discussion which has rarely—if ever—led to any solidarity of action. Doubtless the reason for this lies in the ambiguity of Article 6 of the North Atlantic Treaty but also in the diversity of political commitment on the part of the Allies.

WEU is fortunate in being free from any such ambiguity. The modified Brussels Treaty, the Rome Declaration and the 'Platform on European Security Interests' empower the Member States of WEU to confer together when confronted by threats arising outside the immediate

---

* The sole exception being Iceland.
§ See below, pp. 57-64.

European or allied defence zone which may threaten Europe's security interests, as construed in the perspective of common Atlantic security.

This is significant and has led, in solidarity with the United States, to a first instance of concerted and co-ordinated action by WEU countries in the Gulf. We shall see below how this situation has developed.

The Parliamentary Assembly of WEU

Background

The Parliamentary Assembly was set up in 1954, at the time of the enlargement of the Brussels Treaty to the Federal Republic of Germany and to Italy. Its creation

'was linked with the wishes of the advocates of the European idea to have the same type of democratic representative institutions as in the national framework. In accordance with the principles of parliamentary democracy, the European organisations with political responsibilities should have a representative parliamentary body to balance the governmental representatives'.*

Powers

It is in this spirit that Article IX of the Treaty stipulates that

'The Council of Western European Union shall make an annual report on its activities and in particular concerning the control of armaments to an Assembly composed of representatives of the Brussels Treaty Powers to the Consultative Assembly of the Council of Europe'.

But, in reality, the area of responsibility of the Assembly covered, from the outset, any problem arising out of the modified Brussels Treaty. This possibility was made clear by Mr. Paul-Henri Spaak—then Belgian Foreign Minister and Chairman-in-Office of the WEU Council of Ministers—in a speech given at the first meeting of the

---

* Western European Union, Information Report, submitted on behalf of the Committee for Parliamentary and Public Relations by Mrs. Hennicot-Schoepges, Rapporteur, 17 November 1986.

Assembly on 5 July 1955, in which he said 'We (the Council of WEU) have been determined to leave you the greatest possible freedom, relying upon your experience and wisdom ...'.

Within this framework, the Assembly defined its powers by stating in Article I of its Charter that it could discuss any matter arising out of the modified Brussels Treaty. It also discussed civil and military technological and scientific co-operation and started a dialogue with the Ministerial Council on European political co-operation. In parallel with this, the Assembly has transmitted recommendations to the Council on means of ensuring European security. It felt its actions in this field to be particularly important since it is the only official European parliamentary assembly with competence in defence matters. The WEU Council has always replied to its recommendations, which it may, if it considers it necessary, transmit to the North Atlantic Council.

Membership

As stipulated in Article IX of the modified Brussels Treaty, the WEU Assembly is composed of representatives of the Brussels Treaty Powers to the Consultative Assembly of the Council of Europe, i.e. Belgium, France, the Federal Republic of Germany, Italy, Luxembourg, the Netherlands and the United Kingdom.

Further to Article 26 of the Statute of the Council of Europe, these countries are entitled to the number of representatives given below:

Belgium	7
France	18
Federal Republic of Germany	18
Italy	18
Luxembourg	3
Netherlands	7
United Kingdom	18

The Assembly of WEU is consequently composed of 89 representatives. The same number of 'alternates' is also appointed, all of whom, in practice, are members of their national parliaments, drawn from government and opposition parties, broadly in proportion to the strength of their parties in parliament. Alternates may sit, speak and vote in the place of representatives prevented from attending a sitting of the Assembly. Representatives and alternates may join political groups. There are now four groups: the Communist Group, the Federated Group of Christian Democrats and European Democrats, the Liberal Group and the Socialist Group.

There is currently a debate both within the Assembly and outside, about the composition of the Assembly. We have seen that Article IX of the modified Brussels Treaty provides that the Assembly of the Western European Union is composed of representatives of the Brussels Treaty Powers to the Consultative Assembly of the Council of Europe. As a result, some members of the WEU Assembly may be more interested and competent in matters handled by the Council of Europe than they are in problems dealt with in WEU.

This is why it has been suggested, within the Assembly itself, that Article IX be applied, interpreted or even modified in such a way as to ensure, within the Western European Union Assembly, that the representatives are above all interested in questions of security.

Outside the Assembly—and particularly in the European Parliament—there has been a call for the members of the European Parliament, all of whom are citizens of WEU States, to be the representatives in the WEU Assembly. Speaking at the Hague on 17 March 1988 to the Movement of Young Europeans for Security, the Netherlands Foreign Minister, Mr van den Broek, then Chairman-in-Office of WEU, did not dismiss the possibility that this situation might one day come to pass. Chancellor Kohl, speaking in Brussels on 19 October 1988, has indeed now publicly supported this idea.

An alternative proposal, also originating from the European Parliament, suggested that the Assembly, as presently constituted, should be strengthened by some 50 per cent through the participation of parliamentarians from WEU member countries who were also members of the European Parliament.

As for the WEU Assembly itself, it has considered the idea of reciprocal invitations so that observers from each Assembly could attend each other's meetings. Whatever the outcome of this debate, it must be recognised that, in its present composition—where an effort is made to ensure that members are chosen who are particularly well-versed in defence questions—the Assembly is working hard and producing substantive results.

The Assembly and Other European and Atlantic Parliamentary Fora

As one of its Committees reported in 1986:

The Assembly has always been careful to co-ordinate its action with that of the other European parlimentary assemblies. Although their composition makes it relatively easy to divide work between the WEU Assembly and the Parliamentary Assembly of the Council of Europe, care has to be exercised in choosing dates and places for meetings. The same is not true for the European Parliament whose activities have spread in recent years, particularly since its election by direct universal suffrage, to areas covered by the WEU Assembly. On 1 December 1981, the Assembly therefore adopted Order 55 inviting its President to study with the President of the European Parliament how relations might be organised between the two assemblies.

Thus an exchange of documents and observers has developed between the Committee on Defence Questions and Armaments of the WEU Assembly and a security and disarmament subcommittee of the European Parliament.

The Assembly has also always followed the work of the North Atlantic Assembly. Admittedly it has no official links or relationship with that Assembly, but since there are a few cases of dual mandates and many of the subjects discussed in the two assemblies are almost identical, there would be good reason for improving the co-ordination of their work. The Committee on Defence Questions and Armaments of our Assembly already meets from time to time with the Military Committee of the North Atlantic Assembly'.*

The Assembly During the 'Somnolent' Period

Between 1973 and 1984, when the activities of the intergovernmental organs were considerably reduced, the Assembly remained the most active part of the Organisation. During these ten years, it pursued its

* Western European Union, Information Report, op. cit., p. 48.

efforts to develop a European security dimension and to call for the reactivation of the Organisation.

However, in the absence of an Executive—the Council of Ministers—to which it could address itself, its efforts, though praiseworthy, seemed to be—from 1973 to 1984—relatively fruitless.

However, when governments of the Member States decided to reactivate the WEU, they were indeed inspired by the numerous resolutions passed by the Assembly.

The Role of the Assembly in the Reactivated WEU

The Rome Declaration gives prominence to the Assembly, stating in its Article 9 that

> 'The Ministers recalled the importance of the WEU Assembly which, as the only European parliamentary body mandated by treaty to discuss defence matters, is called upon to play a growing role'.

This was confirmed by the 'Platform on European Security Interests', which states in Article 5 of its Introduction: 'We highly value the continued involvement in this endeavour of the WEU Assembly, which is the only European parliamentary body mandated by treaty to discuss all aspects of security including defence'.

The Present Role of the Assembly

Thanks to the existence of the Assembly, a democratic and public dialogue on security problems is possible at Western European level. Most importantly, since the reactivation of the Organisation, this dialogue has been re-established because the Assembly can now address itself to a Ministerial Council.

It is a fact that growing sections of public opinion in Europe have distanced themselves from the problem of Europe's security considered in the context of common Atlantic security. Proof of this may be found in the mass demonstrations between 1979 and 1985 against the deployment in Europe of Cruise and Pershing missiles. The development of a West European awareness about security by means of democratic discussion of the issue should bring public opinion into closer contact with defence problems in the context of the Alliance and restore the vital consensus in this area.

Of course, the early stage of this renewed dialogue between Parliamentarians and Ministers has not been easy. The fact, however, that it has gained momentum in what has sometimes been a rather difficult atmosphere, due to the fact that the Assembly was impatient to see the reactivation of the WEU assume a quicker pace, does not detract from its importance.

In keeping with the democratic traditions of the seven member States, this Assembly is now acting as a critic of, and stimulus to, the Council of Ministers.

> 'Ever since its creation, the Assembly has helped to shape a European spirit not only among its members but also in the parliaments of the seven countries which signed the Paris Agreements. In many of its recommendations it has emphasized the need to find a European solution to certain problems and has encouraged parliamentarians to approach their governments to ensure that such a solution is found. Thus it endeavours to promote the political will of governments, parliaments and public opinion which is essential for the building of Europe'.*

* Western European Union, Information Report, op. cit., p. 47.

Current Problems of the Western European Union

WEU's Reactivation: The Obstacles

The reactivation of the Organisation met with a number of obstacles which dogged the early years and, more particularly, its activities during 1985 and the first half of 1986. These difficulties involved:

- the sporadic nature of the 'European reflex' among the member States. This is something fairly common to the work of constructing Europe as a whole, whether we are considering the Communities, Political Co-operation or WEU. It simply means that as regards the construction of Europe, it is rare for all the member States to be seeking the same thing, at the same time, with the same intensity. It is clearly difficult, in these circumstances, to carry forward this process at a sustained rate, be it in the field of economic or foreign policy or of security, the latter being WEU's sphere of competence. This difficulty is even more pronounced for a recently reactivated organisation such as Western European Union than it is for other institutions which have been active for much longer.

The following questions relate to that problem:

- the fact that—in addition to sharing common motives—certain member States had their own, not necessarily converging, motives for reactivating Western European Union. It has taken some time to harmonise these and, even today, an effort is still occasionally required;
- the sensitive nature of the subjects addressed: security problems are amongst those which most directly relate to national sovereignty. It is therefore a domain in which one has to proceed with caution;
- the position of Western European Union at the crossroads of the 'Twelve' of the European Communities and the Atlantic Alliance,

which means that, while asserting its personality, it must avoid any harmful duplication;

- the fact that the Organisation had been inactive for ten years. It had to be awoken from its 'sleep' and given new impetus. After all, a car that has been in the garage for a long time does not start first time. Its battery is usually flat and, in order to start the engine, the car must first be pushed hard to get it going. This is what had to be done with WEU, care being taken to ensure that the Seven member States pushed in the same direction.

The First Months

All this largely explains why the WEU took more than 18 months to reassert itself. But there were other reasons, also.

The first was that Western European Union did not possess, at the start of its reactivation, all the inter-governmental organs for joint reflection and concerted action necessary to enable it fully and effectively to carry out its role, particularly its new role of European political co-operation in the field of security. These organs had to be set up gradually and had to learn how to function. As this process began, a second set of problems became apparent.

In the West, WEU is the only institution which operates at the level of both the Ministries and Ministers of Foreign Affairs and Defence and which provides a forum where these Ministers and the members of their administrations can meet and work together. It soon became clear that, despite the similarity of political options, the approach to problems could vary quite considerably between Ministers and Ministries of Foreign Affairs on the one hand and Defence on the other, principally because the working methods were not always the same.

Consequently, it was not enough to set up the inter-governmental organs; their members also had to learn to work together. This has now happened—as we shall see in the next chapter—but it took several months and all the initial interministerial meetings of the new Western European Union (Rome, 4 November 1985 and—despite a substantive communiqué—Venice, 29-30 April 1986) were affected.*

---

* See, for instance, Bridget Bloom's article in *The Financial Times* of 29 April 1986 on the Venice Ministerial Meeting entitled 'Enthusiasm wanes in Europe for reviving the WEU'.

There was also a third reason. Some of the States involved in the reactivation of WEU, though committed to the process, remained somewhat sceptical about the real possibilities for the Organisation and about its ability to develop positively in both the European and Atlantic context. It was not until the Western European Union chalked up its first achievements that this feeling abated.

A Difficult First Task: An Approach to the Strategic Defence Initiative

It was in these conditions that, in 1985, its Ministers gave the Organisation a first mandate appropriate to its new role. It was to study the politico-strategic implications of the Strategic Defence Initiative—which, it will be recalled, was launched by President Reagan in his celebrated speech of 23 March 1983—and also the problems raised by the American offer to the European allies to participate in the SDI research programme.

To carry out this mandate, the new Western European Union set up a Working Group composed of high-level representatives (of the Foreign and Defence Ministries) from the Seven member countries.

But before the Group got down to work in June 1985, two Heads of State or Government of these same member States had already made public pronouncements on the issue, revealing significant nuances in their respective positions. This meant that the circumstances in which the Working Group began its deliberations were not entirely propitious. Consequently, many long months were required before a genuine convergence of views emerged among the seven Governments. It was not until after November 1985 that these ideas came to be set down in three interim reports which culminated in a final report which Ministers were to approve and which successfully reflected that dual perspective of European and Atlantic solidarity which is the hallmark of Western European Union.

During the months of negotiations, however, the media—considering they had been going on for too long—frequently proclaimed that the reactivation of the institution was going to be short lived.

The Current Situation

WEU can now be considered as having been effectively reactivated for some three years. During this period, it has managed to overcome most of the handicaps and difficulties which beset the early months of its revival. Nevertheless, although they may have receded, some of these difficulties are still lurking menacingly in the background and great care must be taken to prevent them re-emerging. Indeed, even today, WEU's existence is not trouble-free.

Principal among the difficulties is the one concerned with the bringing together and restructuring of its administrative organs. For historical reasons, these organs are divided between London and Paris. The Secretariat-General of the Organisation has been located in London since the very beginning. However, when the Brussels Treaty was enlarged in October 1954, to include the Federal Republic of Germany (and Italy), in order to make it possible for the Federal Republic of Germany to join the Atlantic Alliance and NATO, some fears were expressed on the Continent, particularly in France, about the possible rebirth of the German military establishment. In these conditions, some guarantees were offered to alleviate these preoccupations. One of them was a limitation—accepted by Bonn—on its military equipment production. In order to control these restrictions, an Agency for the Control of Armaments was created and located in Paris. A few months later, it was decided to entrust the Organisation with competence in the field of arms co-operation and to create for that purpose a Standing Armaments Committee, also located in Paris.

In 1973, WEU 'went to sleep'. When it woke up, eleven years later, things had changed. There was no fear any more of a rebirth of the German military establishment. The Federal Republic of Germany (FRG) had become an essential element of the Atlantic Alliance and of the process of European construction, and had developed privileged links with France. As a matter of fact—in the framework of WEU's reactivation—practically all the limitations imposed on the FRG in the field of military equipment production were lifted in June 1984.

On the other hand, arms co-operation had developed in another and larger forum, the Independent European Programme Group (IEPG), and was also pursued by the European Communities in the context of the latter's industrial policies. There was therefore no longer any reason to maintain, in the Western European Union, a large Arms Control Agency, and there were grounds for reviewing the role of the Standing Armaments Committee as well as the activities of its Secretariat.

This is why the seven WEU Member States decided, in 1985, when they reactivated the Organisation, to transform this Agency and the Standing Armaments Committee's Secretariat into three 'Agencies'—that is three small 'think-tanks'—devoted to the study, respectively, of problems of arms control negotiations, security and arms co-operation. The three 'think-tanks' would remain in Paris, the idea being to review the whole situation after two years' experience, i.e. in 1987.

On 27 October 1987, the seven governments considered that it would be beneficial to merge the three 'think-tanks' into one, with competence both in security (i.e. arms control negotiations and defence) and defence capabilities (in particular, arms co-operation and the allocation and management of defence resources).

Its staff would be somewhat reduced in comparison with the three former Agencies, while the staff of the Secretariat-General would be reinforced to allow it to meet its growing responsibilities, namely the preparation and conduct of, and follow-up to, an increasing number of meetings of the inter-governmental organs. Thus restructured, the single Agency and the Secretariat-General would be located in a single place under the authority of the Secretary-General who already had administrative control both of his Secretariat-General and of the Agencies.

Since then, however, although the structural changes have gone forward, the question of location has remained unresolved since the governments concerned have not been able to agree on the site of collocation. What is the reason for this failure?

First, the problem is linked to that of the permanent seat of the various European institutions. Although Brussels is host to most of these institutions, three cities continue to vie for the honour of housing them permanently, namely Luxembourg, Strasbourg and of course the Belgian capital. This is one of the reasons why another institution—the European Parliament—still has to divide its activities between the three seats.

Second, because, whereas some member States consider that the proximity of NATO, the European Communities and Political Co-operation among the Twelve makes Brussels an obvious choice, another fears that it would lead to WEU—whose reactivation is still quite recent—being overshadowed by these much larger fora.

Admittedly, this failure does not prevent the Western European Union from progressing and fulfilling its role. But this outstanding problem should be solved; negotiations to that end are in progress.

Current Achievements of WEU and Their Significance for the Alliance and Western Security

In spite of the handicaps we have just enumerated, the reactivation of Western European Union is now a reality. This has been formally recognised by its Foreign and Defence Ministers in their Luxembourg Communiqué of 28 April 1987, in which they state that they 'noted with satisfaction that the reactivation of the Organisation, which allowed for a close association of the Foreign and Defence Ministers, had become a reality'. The Organisation has thus begun to fulfil the role for which its Contracting Parties endeavoured to give it a new lease of life.

Since 1985, it can boast several important achievements.

The Creation of a Continuous Dialogue Among Member States

It has indeed succeeded in setting up a framework for continuous dialogue among the Member States on the problems of European security within the context of joint Atlantic solidarity.

Between 1948 and 1984, WEU had only two inter-governmental organs, i.e.

- a Council of Ministers which brought together the Foreign Ministers approximately twice a year but which did not meet at all during the Organisation's somnolent period between 1973 and 1984;
- a Permanent Council made up of the Ambassadors to the Court of St James's of six member countries and a Representative of the Foreign and Commonwealth Office.

Clearly, these structures were insufficient to create a permanent dialogue between WEU's Member States which could lead to clear conclusions being drawn or firm decisions being taken. For that to happen, it was vital to bring together all those people within the Foreign and Defence Ministries who had the requisite level of responsibility and authority. When these prominent personalities reach common conclusions after a meeting, and once they have returned to their Administrations and given their instructions, the implementation of these conclusions gives rise to converging or common policies and actions.

This is why new inter-governmental organs have been created since WEU's reactivation:

- Ministers meet at least twice a year at the Foreign and Defence level. WEU is the only institution in the West where these Ministers of Foreign Affairs and Defence come together;
- the Political Directors of the Ministries of Foreign Affairs meet periodically, generally with a representative of equivalent rank from the Ministries of Defence. It was decided that they would meet at least four times a year, but in 1987 they did so some eleven times, in view of the number and the importance of the questions they had to address;
- a Special Working Group, comprising the politico-military Directors from the Ministries of Foreign Affairs with, again, a representative of equivalent rank from the Ministries of Defence meets more frequently (in practice about once a month, but quite often three times a month, as in 1987);
- finally, experts, again from both Ministries, also meet to address matters entrusted to them such as the problems raised for Europe by developments in the Strategic Defence Initiative, questions of security in the Mediterranean and problems concerned with the allocation and management of defence resources. The frequency of their meetings is governed by the demands of their work.

These new structures are in addition to the Permanent Council whose task it is to coordinate the Organisation's activities. They constitute the very heart of WEU and the place where converging attitudes among the Member States regarding their security can develop. Between meetings, their members remain in daily contact through a special communications network linking together, in the seven capitals, all the civil servants competent in the field of security.

These inter-governmental organs are assisted by a Secretariat-General whose role is to ensure that meetings are properly prepared, efficiently conducted and followed up. The administrative organisation is light in structure with a small number of officials. This Secretariat is headed by the Secretary-General and based in London.

The Emergence of Converging, or Joint, Positions

This dialogue has been leading to converging or even joint European positions on the numerous security problems daily confronting its Member States.

A feature of the present international situation is a rapid development both in East-West and transatlantic relations. Many local conflicts are also developing and some of them threaten the security interests of the West and of Europe in the widest sense.

This convergence of views enables the WEU member countries to face this international situation together and, to their own benefit, have more influence on events. It has been clearly manifest since the second half of the 1980s in the face of events that are increasing daily. Striking evidence of this was first seen at the Ministerial meeting on 13 and 14 November 1986, in the aftermath of Reykjavík. The joint conclusions reached by the participants enabled them to speak to their allies, and in particular the United States, of their parallel concerns. It is no longer a secret that the British Prime Minister, Margaret Thatcher, used these joint conclusions in her Camp David talks with President Reagan.

Since then, the same phenomenon has occurred in relation to the varying course of East-West disarmament talks. This has not always been an easy matter. But the dialogue, now covering all essential security issues, has continued among our 14 (Foreign and Defence) Ministers and among their immediate collaborators, thus allowing views to be brought closer, harmonised and even jointly expressed in a similar way.

This was clearly demonstrated in the press conference that the Netherlands Ministers of Foreign Affairs and Defence, Mr. van den Broek and Mr. van Eekelen, then Chairmen-in-Office of WEU, gave at the end of the Ministerial Council in The Hague on 18-19 April 1988. Mr. van den Broek told the Press that Ministers had addressed the current major issues relating to arms control and defence requirements from a European perspective and that they had instructed the Special Working Group to study these questions with the aim of harmonising European views. In this way, a more effective European input into Alliance thinking on such issues as the comprehensive concept of arms control and disarmament could be achieved, thereby contributing to a further strengthening of the Alliance as a whole.

Mr. van Eekelen informed the Press of Ministers' decisions to move forward with studying ways of implementing the defence aspects of the Platform. Burden-sharing was another issue discussed at length and, in this respect, Mr. van Eekelen announced that the WEU member countries would keep each other closely informed both prior to and following the visit to several European capitals of a United States delegation headed by the American Deputy-Secretary of Defense, William H. Taft.*

The Development of a European Security Identity

As such converging views, with respect to topical questions in the field of their security, emerged more and more, the seven member States of the Western European Union became increasingly conscious that these convergences were in line with something more fundamental: their longer-term security interests and the options originating from them.

This was, in fact, nothing new or revolutionary. It had, after all, already been recognised, in Alliance context, for instance in the Ottawa Declaration of 1974, adopted by the Ministers of Foreign Affairs. This Declaration, quite naturally, laid down the principle of the unity of the Alliance in the face of the threat to all its members. However, it also emphasized the specific vulnerability of Europe, which thus has a special position—that is special interests—in the context of Atlantic solidarity.

---

* Deputy-Secretary Taft did indeed visit Europe in May 1988. He met most of the European Allied Governments' representatives on the question of 'Burden-sharing'. But he made a point to discuss this problem with the leaders of the Netherlands, not only in their capacity of members of the Dutch Government, but also as acting Presidents of the Western European Union. What is more, he also met with the Secretary-General of the Organisation. This was no doubt an important recognition of the Western European Union by the United States Administration.

However, there had never been any attempt to clarify and define these fundamental joint interests, nor had their consequences been considered. It is a task that WEU has undertaken at the instigation of its member States. It met a need identified in November 1986 in the aftermath of Reykjavík and in the appeal made in December 1986 by the French Prime Minister, Mr. Jacques Chirac, in an address to the Parliamentary Assembly of WEU in which he called for a definition of the 'principles of Western European security'.

Serious and in-depth work was begun and lasted nine months. It resulted in the seven Governments finding considerable common ground in their security interests and options. The fruits of this work were embodied in a report which in turn led to the 'Platform' adopted by the 14 Ministers on 27 October 1987 in The Hague. In adopting this 'Platform', the 'Seven' have begun to fulfil one of the essential roles assigned to them, in the indispensable context of Atlantic solidarity, namely, the definition of some European identity in the security area. This marks an important stage both in the construction of Europe and in the strengthening of a European pillar of the Alliance.

'Out-of-Area' Achievements

As we have already seen, this new European solidarity in the field of security has also shown itself in a region outside the direct defence area of Europe or the Alliance. This occurred in response to the increasing threat to freedom of navigation posed by mine-laying in the Gulf as a result of the Iran/Iraq War.

From August 1987, there was political consultation between our member countries on this subject within WEU. On that basis, but within the framework of national operations, five of them dispatched ships in the region whilst the two others expressed their political solidarity with their partners.

The two in question were the FRG and Luxembourg. Germany is— according to the interpretation it is giving at present to its Basic Law—constitutionally forbidden to take part in such operations. It nevertheless agreed, as necessary, to replace within the Alliance area (not only in the Atlantic Ocean but also in the Mediterranean area, in which it had not been present until then) any of its partners' units that left for the Gulf. Luxembourg made a financial contribution.

The national operations were technically co-ordinated—under WEU's aegis—both on the spot and at Admiralty level. These European forces in the Gulf were, moreover, side by side with the American ones.

During 1989 and 1988, regular meetings took place which resulted in a three-tier framework of political concertation and practical co-operation:

— discussions between Foreign and Defense Ministers and their senior officials
— meetings between the naval staffs in the capitals
— regular consultation between naval commanders on the spot.

Let us see what Minister van Eekelen said, in this respect, on 19 April 1988, at the Press Conference concluding the WEU Ministerial Council and which has been quoted above:

'... We have noted that our practical arrangements within the WEU framework have been justified, are workable and have been put into practice, because in this operation, for the first time, not only the Belgian/Netherlands unit under joint command and in close tactical coordination with the British frigates has been operating successfully, but in that same operation also British mine-hunters and Italian mine-hunters have been active and an Italian frigate has extended its protection to the whole fleet of vessels, at present. So from a European point of view, I think it is a successful operation, especially in showing that our combined operations are workable.

Now, what are we going to do for the next few months? In the first place, we have decided to intensify our discussions, a new assessment is now necessary as far as the mine threat is concerned, but of course the overall situation in the Gulf will be further reviewed ...'.

In the same context, Minister van den Broek underlined:

'(...) the grave concern of the members of WEU at the recent increase in hostilities in the Gulf following the new mining activities, and attacks against merchant shipping in the area', adding 'We

PLATE 3: Ships of WEU nations on patrol in the Gulf. 1987

thought it opportune to stress again the necessity of respecting the principle of free navigation. Several members of WEU contribute to the safeguarding of these rights by their maritime presence in the Gulf and we underlined again the importance of such a contribution to the maintenance of freedom of navigation. Furthermore, Ministers have clearly called for an immediate end to all mining and other hostile activities against shipping in international waters, taking into account, as the statement reads, that such activities can call for measures of self-defence. Well, it goes without saying that the present developments in the Gulf that give great concern are in fact the symptoms of a conflict which needs to be addressed in its hard core, and therefore WEU members have stated they will continue their diplomatic efforts, particularly within the framework of European political co-operation, to support all endeavours towards the full and early implementation of resolution 598 of the Security Council (since) this resolution is the only framework for an overall resolution to the problems raised by the Iran/Iraq conflict'.

Practical co-operation was taken a step further with the signing of a memorandum on 1 July 1988 setting up a common operational command between the ships of the UK, Belgium and the Netherlands.

After the cease-fire was concluded in the Gulf War in July 1988, WEU took responsibility for concerting its members' mine counter-measures forces in a major operation to clear mines from the lower Gulf. This operation—'Cleansweep'—was a fitting culmination to a major pioneering landmark in European naval co-operation.

As the threat to freedom of navigation receded towards the end of 1988, so the member countries took decisions to reduce or withdraw entirely their naval forces from the Gulf.

The success of the Gulf exercise has demonstrated that WEU can act as an effective European forum for establishing political concertation and practical co-operation between member countries in crisis situations where their security interests are affected.

The Enlargement of the Western European Union

New Members?

Since 1954, there have been seven members of WEU. The success of its reactivation has, however, aroused the attention of other States. In October 1984, Portugal, followed in 1985 by Spain, showed interest in joining the Organisation. Since then, Greece and Turkey have done likewise.

The modified Brussels Treaty makes express provision for the accession of new countries to the Organisation as its Article XI stipulates:

> 'The High Contracting Parties may, by agreement, invite any other State to accede to the present Treaty on conditions to be agreed between them and the State so invited ...'.

Moreover, the Seven have always said that they did not want to form a 'closed shop' and intended to open their Organisation, at the appropriate moment, to other European countries, provided that they shared their democratic regime and politico-strategic options.

At the same time, they do not wish enlargement to damage the Organisation's cohesion. This was why they decided to advance cautiously along this road and, in particular, to wait until WEU had been fully reactivated before issuing the first invitations.

The Criteria for Possible Accession

What conditions must a State fulfil to be invited to accede to WEU?

From the 'Platform' it is clear that a State must be a member of the Atlantic Alliance, but not necessarily of NATO's integrated structure, to which one of its present member States—France—is not party.

Obviously, the candidate country must fully accept the modified Brussels Treaty, the contents of the Rome Declaration and of the

'Platform'. In this connection, it will normally be required to stipulate during preparatory negotiations how it intends to be part of the European security identity, to show its solidarity with its partners and to make its contribution to European security, considered in the context of common Atlantic security.

It must also subscribe to the process of building Europe. Does this mean that it must be one of the twelve members of the European Communities and Political Co-operation? The 'Platform' suggests that this is so when it states:

> 'We (the Member States) recall our commitment to build a European Union in accordance with the Single European Act, which we all signed as members of the European Community (...)'.

However, this point is not unanimously agreed upon by the present Member States, some of which—in the event, for instance, that Norway might show interest in WEU—would not wish such a condition necessarily to form an obstacle to that country's possible accession to the Organisation.

The Overlapping Circles: WEU, EC, NATO

One of the obvious questions is whether the Western European Union—with its characteristics as an element of European construction and its objective of forming a European pillar of the Alliance—could one day encompass either all the members of the European Communities and European Political Co-operation, or all the European members of the Alliance.

We have seen earlier* that, with respect to the European construction, it was precisely because three member States of what were then the 'Ten' could not accept, at this stage, the development, in this context, of a full European security dimension that the Western European Union was reactivated. They were Denmark, Greece and Ireland. It seems that Greece's position had undergone a shift but neither Denmark nor Ireland appear to have changed their position.

---

* See above, pp. 8-16.

As for the NATO countries, these must not only meet the conditions listed above but also wish to join WEU. Though this is the case with Turkey and Greece, it is not *at present* the case of other countries, particularly Denmark and Norway, though their contribution to the common defence of the Northern flank of Europe is very significant.

In any event, the aim of the seven member States of Western European Union is to adopt a step-by-step procedure which will ensure that, whilst expanding, WEU should not lose any of its rediscovered vigour and should remain a homogenous unit.

Portugal and Spain

After three years of effort, the Western European Union has finally been effectively reactivated. This was recognized by the Luxembourg Ministerial Communiqué of 28 April 1987* and was made clear by the adoption of the 'Platform on European Security Interests'.

Under these circumstances, a cautious first step towards the enlargement of the Organisation was possible. Consequently, it was decided by the WEU Ministers in April 1988 to send an invitation to the first countries to have shown an interest to join the Organisation, Portugal and Spain, to begin discussions with a view to their possible accession to WEU.

They agreed to the following terms in which to invite Portugal and Spain to start these negotiations:

> 'The Council of Ministers of WEU has taken note of the fact that Portugal and Spain, which are fully committed to the process of European construction and are members of the Atlantic Alliance, have formally stated that they are prepared to accede to the modified Brussels Treaty and accept unreservedly and in their entirety the Rome Declaration of 27 October 1984 and the 'Platform' adopted in The Hague on 27 October 1987 and that they are prepared to participate fully in their implementation.
>
> Consequently, the Council of Ministers of WEU has decided to invite, in conformity with Article XI of the modified Brussels

* See above, pp. 43-50.

Treaty, Portugal and Spain to open the appropriate discussions with a view to their possible accession'.

The separate negotiations with Portugal and Spain were opened in The Hague on 26 May 1988 and continued in London when the United Kingdom took over the Presidency of WEU on 1 July. The process consisted of a series of detailed discussions on substantative political-military issues as well as on certain necessary legal matters.

The discussions were led to a successful conclusion at the Ministerial Meeting in London on 14 November when the Nine countries signed the Protocol of Accession of Portugal and Spain to WEU (see Appendix IV).

The discussions had confirmed that Portugal and Spain accepted the obligations arising from the modified Brussels Treaty—subject to a reserve by Spain on Article X—and that they accepted unreservedly and in their entirety the Rome Declaration and Hague Platform and were prepared to participate fully in their implementation.

It was on this basis that the Nine set out the framework for their future joint action within WEU, a framework that was given clear expression in the Preamble to the Protocol of Accession in which the Nine:

- reaffirmed the common destiny which bound them together and recalled their commitment to build a European union in accordance with the Single European Act;
- stressed their conviction that the construction of an integrated Europe would remain incomplete as long as it did not include security and defence;
- affirmed their determination to develop a more cohesive European defence identity which would translate more effectively into practice the obligation of solidarity contained in the modified Brussels Treaty.

Welcoming Portugal and Spain into WEU, the Chairman-in-Office, Sir Geoffrey Howe, summed up the results of the discussions in the following way:

- both countries emphasized that they shared their partners' common perception, both of European values and of the threat and that they saw the Alliance as the fundamental instrument of Europe's collective defence now and in the future;

PLATE 4: Spain and Portugal signing the Protocol of Accession at the Ministerial Council in London 14 November 1988

- they both subscribed unreservedly, in Spain's case since the 1986 referendum, to the Communiqués of the Alliance;
- they both believed that there was no alternative, for the foreseeable future, to a strategy of defence and effective deterrence based on an adequate mix of nuclear and conventional forces;
- they were both actively engaged in restructuring their armed forces and recognised the need to maintain an adequate level of defence spending;
- they both accepted the commitment to defend any member country at its borders.

Following the signature of the Protocol of Accession, the Foreign and Defence Ministers of Portugal and Spain joined their fourteen colleagues for the continuation of the Ministerial Meeting. It was agreed, pending ratification of the Protocol by all nine parliaments, that Portugal and Spain would take part in all WEU activities as 'active observers'.

European Co-operation in the Field of Security: Towards a 'European Pillar'?

Need for a European Pillar of the Alliance

The old idea of developing a European pillar of the Atlantic Alliance is one which now has renewed topicality and even urgency. The idea was coined and made famous by President J. F. Kennedy. Perhaps at the time when the American Head of State expressed this idea, the problem was not perceived in the same terms as it is today. Yet the idea is even more valid now as a means of responding to new and changing situations, particularly in the context of transatlantic relations.

This vital need is being articulated with increasing forcefulness on both sides of the Atlantic. An example is the report prepared for the North Atlantic Assembly by a group of fifteen parliamentarians from ten allied States and chaired by the United States Senator, William Roth. Entitled 'NATO in the 1990s'*, the report puts forward, inter alia, the proposals that the European members of the Alliance should:

- On an annual basis, prepare a European security assessment identifying the threats to the Western democracies and detailing how they intend to respond to those threats;
- initiate a study of institutional changes that the establishment of a real European pillar in the Alliance would imply, and especially the place and role that the Western European Union (WEU) and the European Economic Community (EEC) would have in building this pillar;
- seek to form a European division based on the forces of a number of European countries that could serve as a special covering force for the Alliance to provide flexibility in responding to a crisis;

* 'NATO in the 1990s', Special Report of the North Atlantic Assembly, Belgium, May 1988.

- develop routine meetings of the military Chiefs of Staff of West European NATO governments and establish a computerised communications network linking planning staffs in European Defence Ministries in order to foster more thorough military co-operation at the European level;
- intensify efforts to create a European-scale defence market;
- encourage task specialization as a means of eliminating wasteful duplication and overlap among national military efforts.

The idea has also been taken up by François Heisbourg, Director of the International Institute for Strategic Studies, in a recent article in *The Times*:

'Today, as in previous decades, the defence of Western Europe and of the United States is difficult to conceive without a substantial physical US conventional and nuclear force in Europe within the framework of a political-strategic alliance. The lessons of geography—Western Europe's lack of strategic depth—and of history—the cost of late US intervention in the First and Second World Wars—point in that direction. But this is only a necessary condition for European and American security, not a sufficient one: a successful future for the Atlantic Alliance depends on a higher degree of European involvement in defining and creating the conditions of its own security within the Alliance. This is true *vis-à-vis* the United States, whose military resources are spread thin and whose public opinion clearly expects an enhanced European role. The same applies to Western Europe, where the unease created by American conduct at the Reykjavík summit and its aftermath combines with the understandable desire for a greater say in security affairs. This is where the gradual building-up of a European pillar can contribute to the regeneration of the Atlantic Alliance. The rationale for such a pillar could be summarized as follows:

—as an instrument for improving and unifying European defence efforts within the Alliance it could contribute to a better balance in terms of burden-sharing and compensate, at least in part, for US force reductions;
—as a means of providing a unified European response in the

face of Soviet attempts to split the European allies it would consolidate the political base of the Alliance, not least in West Germany which is at the centre of this challenge;

— last but not least, the European pillar would be a logical corollary to ventures leading to the creation of a single, unified European market after 1992, not unlike the US continental-scale market.'*

As for David Greenwood, Director of the Centre for Defence Studies of the University of Aberdeen (Scotland), he writes in the *NATO Review*:

'It depends on whether you like your metaphors psychological or architectural. Should the West European members of NATO be cultivating a distinctive identity within the Alliance; or should they be building (or strengthening) a European pillar? The concrete expression is the better of the two. Sometimes identity is all in the mind. Moreover, while you can certainly acquire a new sense of identity, you can also lose it again. But a solid pillar is real; and it is not likely to be here today, gone tomorrow. The true reason for the preference, though, is that Western Europe now really does need to develop not just a more assertive personality when dealing with the affairs of its hemisphere, but also substantial and durable structures of intra-European co-operation to enable it to act coherently and effectively in those dealings. In fact, the future well-being of the Atlantic partnership depends upon it. If this liaison (the Alliance) is to last, therefore, it must mature into a more equal partnership wherever possible'.§

Examples of European Co-operation in the Field of Security

There are a growing number of co-operative ventures among European allies. The phenomenon has both a bilateral and multilateral aspect to it. At bilateral level, the number of co-operative agreements in the field of defence is increasing. The striking example is, of course, the special

---

* *The Times* 8 July 1988, 'Europe's own NATO pillar'.
§ David Greenwood, 'Constructing the European Pillar: Issues and Institutions', published in *NATO Review* No. 3, June 1988, p. 13.

defence relationship between France and the Federal Republic of Germany. It is, after all, only natural and logical that this relationship should be the most impressive. After three Franco-German conflicts the last two of which with great loss of life, were part of world wars, this special relationship has something miraculous about it and without it, ie: without the complete reconciliation on which it is based, progress along the road of European construction would be inconceivable and Atlantic solidarity in doubt.

Yet this Franco-German relationship is far from being the only one of its kind. Many others have developed and new ones are continually emerging. Suffice it to quote the example of the relationship which has been established between the United Kingdom and the Federal Republic of Germany. Though less 'visible' than the Franco-German relationship (and incidentally known as 'The quiet relationship'), it has no less substance. Commendably informative on this subject is a book written by Karl Kaiser and John Roper entitled '*British-German Defence Co-operation—Partners within the Alliance*'.*

At the time of writing, the latest example of these bilateral co-operation arrangements in the field of security between European allies is the Italian-Spanish one which resulted from the Italian-Spanish Summit of 11 July 1988.

At the multilateral level, a distinction should be made between:

- Western European Union
- the organisations which, within the Alliance, are specific to the European allies
- Europe of the Twelve.

The specifically European activities developed within the Alliance are essentially the province of Eurogroup and the Independent European Programme Group.

The Eurogroup was established in 1968 and aims to ensure that the contribution which its twelve members make to Alliance defence is as strong and cohesive as possible. It lays special stress on promoting practical co-operation and has technical sub-groups working in the fields of:

---

* '*British-German Defence Co-operation—Partners within the Alliance*', by Karl Kaiser and John Roper, London 1988, published by Jane's for the Royal Institute of International Affairs (London) and *Forschungsinstitut der Deutschen Gesellschaft für Auswärtige Politik* (Bonn).

- training (EURO/NATOTRAINING)
- logistics (EUROLOG)
- communications (EUROCOM)
- military medicine (EUROMED)
- operational concepts (EUROLONGTERM)

The Defence Ministers of the Eurogroup members meet every six months to direct this activity and to discuss major defence and security issues, especially those related to NATO's defence planning business. The Eurogroup also seeks to explain the European defence effort to audiences in the United States.*

The Independent European Programme Group (IEPG) was established in 1976 to promote European co-operation in the research, development and production of defence equipment, to improve transatlantic armaments co-operation and to help maintain a healthy European industrial and technological defence base. In 1984, the Defence Ministers of the thirteen member nations took over the direction of the IEPG and since then they have met about once a year. This has given fresh impetus to the group's work and good progress is now being made.§

The members of Eurogroup are Belgium, Denmark, the Federal Republic of Germany, Greece, Italy, Luxembourg, the Netherlands, Norway, Portugal, Spain, Turkey and the United Kingdom. The IEPG members are all these plus France.

As for Europe of the Twelve, we have seen earlier** that the Paris Treaty setting up the Coal and Steel Community and the Treaties of Rome establishing the European Economic Community and Euratom had an overall political objective which does not ultimately exclude security. This explains the entirely reasonable and laudable initiatives taken by the President of the European Commission, Mr. Jacques Delors, in this connection. Aware of the current obstacles, however, he had—for the time being at least—placed his hopes in Western European Union as regards the development of a European security dimension.

Be that as it may, the European Economic Community can, within the framework of its industrial policy, already play a part in defining

---

* *Western Defence: The European Role in NATO*, Brussels, May 1988, p. 5.
§ *Western Defence: The European Role in NATO*, op. cit., p. 5.
** See above, pp. 8-16.

and implementing European measures aimed at the armaments (especially conventional) and military equipment industries. It has been doing this for some years and is continuing to do so.

Admittedly, Article 223 of the Rome Treaty excludes armaments from the Common Market. Some people are wondering, however, if the Single European Act, adopted in December 1985 and giving the Communities competence with regard to the economic aspects of security, and the prospect of a single market in 1992, might not combine to alter this state of affairs.

The European Parliament will continue to be a focus for a growing debate on security. Some of its members have already published strong opinions on its future role. See Appendix V for a stimulating paper on 'Collective Security: The European Community and the Preservation of Peace' by Michael Welsh MEP, a member of the European Democratic Group. The paper demonstrates the strength of the convictions of a growing body of opinion in the European Parliament. European Political Co-operation will also continue to provide a potential centre for the development of a European security dimension within the framework of the Community. Until it does so, however, WEU must remain the main vehicle for advancing the European defence identity.

The Impact on NATO

Clearly there is a question mark over whether this multiplicity of intra-European co-operative arrangements, both bilateral and multilateral, is not confusing or even divisive for the Alliance. In reality the opposite is true and what has happened in practice is that—though there may occasionally be one or two minor 'failures'—these co-operative ventures among European allies offer the prospect of valuable solidarity which both profits and strengthens the Alliance. Obviously, it is vital so that this should continue to be the case, that the three conditions mentioned earlier*, namely compatibility, transparency and enhanced commitment, should be scrupulously adhered to by the various forms of intra-European co-operation in their relationships with the Alliance.

This is what is happening in practice and, because of it, a gradual

* See above, pp. 17-26.

change is taking place which is making the European allies more and more interdependent, both among themselves and within the Alliance, for the greater good of the latter. When France, for example, together with its six partners in WEU, proclaims its willingness 'to make clearly manifest by means of appropriate arrangements its determination to defend any member country (of WEU) at its borders', that does not mean that it is returning to the NATO integrated structure or even that it is participating in implementing NATO's strategy of forward defence. What it does mean is, however, that it is committing itself to taking additional measures to fulfil the obligation to which it subscribes. Joint Franco-German manoeuvres such as the 'Cheeky Sparrow' Exercise are clearly part of this approach.

President Reagan also recognised this co-operation in his speech of 4 November 1987 when he said:

'And let there be no doubt, the citizens of the United States fully understand and appreciate that we are partners for peace with you, the people of our fellow Western democracies. That is why we applaud what we see as a new willingness, even eagerness, on the part of our allies to increase the level of co-operation and co-ordination among themselves in European defence. The growing co-operation between France and Germany is a positive sign, as is the modernization of the British and the French independent nuclear deterrents, which are both vital components of the Western security system'.

The Special Role of WEU

By being complementary in their activities, these various European co-operative ventures are helping to lay the foundations for a European pillar of the Alliance. Obviously, additional efforts are required for it to develop further.

A question which has repeatedly been put and is still being asked, however, is whether this development could not be brought about more effectively within the context of a single forum. It is with this in mind that a number of people have suggested that the efforts of the European allies to construct their pillar within the Alliance should for example focus on the Eurogroup or the IEPG.

But the IEPG—which plays an essential role in the area of European arms co-operation—has no general competence in the field of security. Eurogroup, though comprising twelve European members of the Alliance, does not include Iceland and above all France. France, by contrast, is one of the members of WEU, whose members number only seven—now nine—European allies. Consequently, Western European Union is the only framework in which the British, Germans, Italians, Dutch, Luxembourgers and Belgians (and now also the Portuguese and Spanish) can discuss defence on a multilateral basis with their French ally, at the level of both Foreign and Defence Ministers.

What is more, the Western European Union is the only European organisation to have a Parliamentary Assembly which is the sole European parliamentary body formally mandated to discuss security and defence matters. In these conditions, how does this WEU fit in with the other centres of co-operation among European allies?

Anxious to contribute through its action to the strengthening of the Alliance and to progress in the process of European construction, the Organisation endeavours to avoid any activity which might impede the activities of the other centres of co-operation and is at pains to avoid any harmful duplication.

That said, it is seeking to assert itself more and more as a spokesman for Europe in the field of security and in the framework of Atlantic solidarity. Its 'Platform on European security interests' is evidence of this, as was the co-ordinated presence, under its aegis, of naval vessels from five of its member States in the Gulf.

That point has been very clearly made by the United Kingdom Foreign Secretary, Sir Geoffrey Howe, when he referred to the Organisation as

'The arch between NATO's two pillars', whose aim is 'to bring a clearer European thinking in the Alliance' and to be 'a necessary vehicle if the Europeans are to contribute more to their own defence—in ideas as well as in substance'.*

It was confirmed by David Greenwood:

'There can be no sound European pillar within the Atlantic Alliance without a sound policy bloc. Furthermore, this foundation must be put in place early. Unless cast in the WEU mould it is likely to be neither'.§

* Speech delivered at the *Institut Royal des Relations Internationales*, Brussels, 16 March 1987.
§ David Greenwood, *'Constructing the European Pillar: Issues and Institutions'*, op. cit., p. 15.

Conclusion: Tasks Ahead

The Problem of European Security in a Changing International Environment

The Western European security environment remained static throughout the 1970s and early 1980s with regard to

- Developments in the USSR,
- The evolution of East-West relations and
- The transatlantic relationship.

In the Soviet Union, the last three years of General-Secretary Brezhnev's reign were characterised by a rigid immobilism which—after General-Secretary Andropov's short-lived leadership—was quietly and steadfastly pursued by General-Secretary Chernenko.

This certainly did not necessarily favour positive developments in the field of East-West relations. This was clearly demonstrated by the events between 1976 and 1985, which marked the end of the so-called 'détente period' and by the progressive return to an atmosphere that was growing colder. But it did lend to this relationship between Moscow on the one hand, and Washington and its Atlantic allies on the other, a predictability which was doubtless not very constructive but nevertheless quite comfortable.

As far as the transatlantic relationship is concerned, it is a fact that it lived through the late 1970s and early 1980s in a situation of *status quo*. Of course, there were problems like those created in Europe by some significant popular opposition to the deployment of Cruise missiles and Pershing II in accordance with the Allies' dual-track decision of December 1979. But such problems did not prevent things from remaining essentially the same in the Alliance. Admittedly, *status quo* is not a very dynamic position to be in, but it is a rather comfortable one to which an Alliance easily becomes accustomed.

Today, this static context, in which our Western European security had found itself for so many years, has become a thing of the past. What is more, events have moved on at such a pace that it feels like ages since it disappeared. It has abruptly disintegrated and given way to entirely new and rapidly-evolving situations.

In Moscow, rigid immobilism has been replaced by a dynamic policy some aspects of which—particularly in the sphere of external relations and security—may appear to be tactical but which nevertheless have considerable importance and true substance. In addition, this new 'thaw' in the Soviet Union has had an impact on the other Warsaw Pact countries where we see—at government level—a tendency to assert themselves nationally, at European level and even on the wider international plane. We also note the concern of the same governments at the awakening of public opinion to which their response is either cautious liberalisation or a sudden hardening of attitudes.

In any event, these changes have visible or even spectacular consequences for East-West relations, particularly in the sphere of arms control negotiations where there is a new surge of activity. All these developments are, of course, part of the reason for the end of the state of somnolence in which the Atlantic Alliance had lived for many years and, in that respect, the Reykjavík Summit of October 1986 was undoubtedly something of a turning point.

But these factors are not the only ones which have led to the end of the *status quo* in the Alliance. Another no less important one is the growing debate on both sides of the Atlantic about the future of the transatlantic relationship. In the face of rapidly-evolving East-West relations and of a transatlantic relationship clearly in transition, the Allies are finding it more necessary than ever to strengthen both their solidarity and, in a changing world, to spell out its terms. In this respect, Europeans have responsibilities to shoulder and a role to play.

To do so, it is essential that they get their act together. If they fail, they will increasingly become spectators and not actors in an international situation, the developments in which would increasingly pass them by. There could then be a risk of seeing the different European States reacting in a random fashion, and even adopting divergent positions and policies. This would lead to a 'dilution' or an 'implosion' of the European construction process. It would also lead to the progressive and possibly rapid disintegration of the Alliance.

If, on the contrary, West Europeans come closer together with the will both to shoulder their share of the common defence effort and to exercise their share of influence, they will at the same time ensure progress in the construction of Europe and contribute to maintaining Atlantic cohesion.

It must be emphasized that these two objectives are not contradictory. In reality, the construction of a more united Europe and the strengthening of the Alliance are in fact complementary.

The experience of the last three years, of the results achieved during this period by the reactivated Western European Union show that WEU can help achieve that. The Organisation has in fact begun to establish a European security identity. This is not a question of a European defence, since at the present time, it is inconceivable to consider the defence of Western Europe outside the essential framework of the Alliance. What is at issue is a European security and defence identity with all that this implies in terms of awareness of these issues among public opinion.

Such an identity fits perfectly into the context of building a more united Europe which can then develop a security dimension. It is also within the context of the Atlantic Alliance where it strengthens the commitment, contribution and role of Western Europe—the essential second pillar of the Atlantic world.

The Way Forward

It is in this context that, in the coming months, the Organisation will give priority to the following tasks:

- to elaborate the commitments in the WEU Platform and, where possible, use them as a means of encouraging better practical contributions to the common defence;
- to use the WEU as a forum for concerting views on topical issues in the security and arms control field in order to provide a more coherent European input to Alliance discussions;
- to develop the WEU as a forum for co-ordinating its members' approaches to out-of-area issues.

In the longer term—and in any case as long as no progress is possible within the Twelve—Western European Union will have to assert itself as the 'Security Component' of the European construction process. This means that its action must be both deepened and expanded.

In the words of the President of the European Commission, Jacques Delors, this component should provide an 'interface' between the European Community, European Political Co-operation and the Atlantic Alliance. At the same time, a new WEU will strive more vigorously than in the past to set its activities in the context of the Alliance and in that of Atlantic solidarity.

Within this Organisation, a growing cohesion among its members should enable them to assume their responsibilities as allies with growing effectiveness, be this in the immediate zone of Atlantic defence or outside it, whenever European security interests are threatened. Obviously, this is a long-haul undertaking. There is a long way to go and the path is strewn with obstacles. But we know that the building of a united Europe is a dynamic process which not only demands boldness and breadth of vision but also effort on a day-to-day basis.

That great European, Jean Monnet, knew this better than anyone when he said, at the end of his 'Mémoires' that

'those unwilling to undertake anything because they had no guarantee that things would turn out as they had planned were doomed to paralysis. No one today can predict the shape of the Europe of tomorrow, for it is impossible to foretell what changes will be begotten by change (...) The path ahead must be opened up a day at a time, the most important thing being to have an objective clear enough not to be lost sight of.'*

* Jean Monnet, *Mémoires*, Fayard 1976, p. 616.

Appendix I
The Brussels Treaty
and Protocols

TREATY OF ECONOMIC, SOCIAL AND
CULTURAL COLLABORATION AND COLLECTIVE
SELF-DEFENCE SIGNED AT BRUSSELS ON
MARCH 17, 1948, AS AMENDED BY THE
'PROTOCOL MODIFYING AND COMPLETING
THE BRUSSELS TREATY'
Signed at Paris on October 23, 1954

(The High Contracting Parties)

Resolved:

To reaffirm their faith in fundamental human rights, in the dignity and worth of the human person and in the other ideals proclaimed in the Charter of the United Nations;

To fortify and preserve the principles of democracy, personal freedom and political liberty, the constitutional traditions and the rule of law, which are their common heritage;

To strengthen, with these aims in view, the economic, social and cultural ties by which they are already united;

To co-operate loyally and to co-ordinate their efforts to create in Western Europe a firm basis for European economic recovery;

To afford assistance to each other, in accordance with the Charter of the United Nations, in maintaining international peace and security and in resisting any policy of aggression;

To promote the unity and to encourage the progressive integration of Europe;

To associate progressively in the pursuance of these aims other States inspired by the same ideals and animated by the like determination;

Desiring for these purposes to conclude a treaty of collaboration in economic, social and cultural matters and for collective self-defence;

Have agreed as follows:

ARTICLE I

Convinced of the close community of their interests and of the necessity of uniting in order to promote the economic recovery of Europe, the High Contracting Parties will so organise and co-ordinate their economic activities as to produce the best possible results, by the elimination of conflict in their economic policies, the co-ordination of production and the development of commercial exchanges.

The co-operation provided for in the preceding paragraph, which will be effected through the Council referred to in Article VIII, as well as through other bodies, shall not involve any duplication of, or prejudice to, the work of other economic organisations in which the High Contracting Parties are or may be represented, but shall on the contrary assist the work of those organisations.

ARTICLE II

The High Contracting Parties will make every effort in common, both by direct consultation and in specialised agencies, to promote the attainment of a higher standard of living by their peoples and to develop on corresponding lines the social and other related services of their countries.

The High Contracting Parties will consult with the object of achieving the earliest possible application of recommendations of immediate practical interest, relating to social matters, adopted with their approval in the specialised agencies.

They will endeavour to conclude as soon as possible conventions with each other in the sphere of social security.

ARTICLE III

The High Contracting Parties will make every effort in common to lead their peoples towards a better understanding of the principles which form the basis of their common civilisation and to promote cultural exchanges by conventions between themselves or by other means.

ARTICLE IV

In the execution of the Treaty, the High Contracting Parties and any Organs established by Them under the Treaty shall work in close co-operation with the North Atlantic Treaty Organisation.

Recognising the undesirability of duplicating the military staffs of NATO, the Council and its Agency will rely on the appropriate military authorities of NATO for information and advice on military matters.

ARTICLE V

If any of the High Contracting Parties should be the object of an armed attack in Europe, the other High Contracting Parties will, in accordance with the provisions of Article 51 of the Charter of the United Nations, afford the Party so attacked all the military and other aid and assistance in their power.

ARTICLE VI

All measures taken as a result of the preceding Article shall be immediately reported to the Security Council. They shall be terminated as soon as the Security Council has taken the measures necessary to maintain or restore international peace and security.

The present Treaty does not prejudice in any way the obligations of the High Contracting Parties under the provisions of the Charter of the United Nations. It shall not be interpreted as affecting in any way the authority and responsibility of the Security Council under the Charter to take at any time such action as it deems necessary in order to maintain or restore international peace and security.

ARTICLE VII

The High Contracting Parties declare, each so far as he is concerned, that none of the international engagements now in force between him and any other of the High Contracting Parties or any third State is in conflict with the provisions of the present Treaty.

None of the High Contracting Parties will conclude any alliance or participate in any coalition directed against any other of the High Contracting Parties.

ARTICLE VIII

1. For the purposes of strengthening peace and security and of promoting

unity and of encouraging the progressive integration of Europe and closer co-operation between Them and with other European organisations, the High Contracting Parties to the Brussels Treaty shall create a Council to consider matters concerning the execution of this Treaty and of its Protocols and their Annexes.

2. This Council shall be known as the "Council of Western European Union"; it shall be so organised as to be able to exercise its functions continuously; it shall set up such subsidiary bodies as may be considered necessary: in particular it shall establish immediately an Agency for the Control of Armaments whose functions are defined in Protocol No. IV.

3. At the request of any of the High Contracting Parties the Council shall be immediately convened in order to permit them to consult with regard to any situation which may constitute a threat to peace, in whatever area this threat should arise, or a danger to economic stability.

4. The Council shall decide by unanimous vote questions for which no other voting procedure has been or may be agreed. In the cases provided for in Protocols II, III and IV it will follow the various voting procedures, unanimity, two-thirds majority, simple majority, laid down therein. It will decide by simple majority questions submitted to it by the Agency for the Control of Armaments.

ARTICLE IX

The Council of Western European Union shall make an annual report on its activities and in particular concerning the control of armaments to an Assembly composed of representatives of the Brussels Treaty Powers to the Consultative Assembly of the Council of Europe.

ARTICLE X

In pursuance of their determination to settle disputes only by peaceful means, the High Contracting Parties will apply to disputes between themselves the following provisions;

The High Contracting Parties will, while the present Treaty remains in force, settle all disputes falling within the scope of Article 36, paragraph 2, of the Statute of the International Court of Justice, by referring them to the Court, subject only, in the case of each of them, to any reservation already made by that Party when accepting this clause for compulsory jurisdiction to the extent that that Party may maintain the reservation.

In addition, the High Contracting Parties will submit to conciliation all disputes outside the scope of Article 36, paragraph 2, of the Statute of the International Court of Justice.

In the case of a mixed dispute involving both questions for which conciliation is appropriate and other questions for which judicial settlement is appropriate, any Party to the dispute shall have the right to insist that the judicial settlement of the legal questions shall precede conciliation.

The preceding provisions of this Article in no way affect the application of relevant provisions or agreements prescribing some other method of pacific settlement.

ARTICLE XI

The High Contracting Parties may, by agreement, invite any other State to accede to the present Treaty on conditions to be agreed between them and the State so invited.

Any State so invited may become a Party to the Treaty by depositing an instrument of accession with the Belgian Government.

The Belgian Government will inform each of the High Contracting Parties of the deposit of each instrument of accession.

ARTICLE XII

The present Treaty shall be ratified and the instruments of ratification shall be deposited as soon as possible with the Belgian Government.

It shall enter into force on the date of the deposit of the last instrument of ratification and shall thereafter remain in force for fifty years.

After the expiry of the period of fifty years, each of the High Contracting Parties shall have the right to cease to be a party thereto provided that he shall have previously given one year's notice of denunciation to the Belgian Government.

The Belgian Government shall inform the Governments of the other High Contracting Parties of the deposit of each instrument of ratification and of each notice of denunciation.

PROTOCOL MODIFYING AND COMPLETING THE BRUSSELS TREATY

Signed at Paris on October 23, 1954;
entered into force on May 6, 1955

His Majesty the King of the Belgians, the President of the French Republic, President of the French Union, Her Royal Highness the Grand Duchesss of Luxembourg, Her Majesty the Queen of the Netherlands and Her Majesty the Queen of the United Kingdom of Great Britain and Northern Ireland and of Her other Realms and Territories, Head of the Commonwealth, Parties to the Treaty of Economic, Social and Cultural Collaboration and Collective Self-Defence, signed at Brussels on March 17, 1948, hereinafter referred to as the Treaty, on the one hand,

and the President of the Federal Republic of Germany and the President of the Italian Republic on the other hand,

Inspired by a common will to strengthen peace and security;

Desirous to this end of promoting the unity and of encouraging the progressive integration of Europe;

Convinced that the accession of the Federal Republic of Germany and the Italian Republic to the Treaty will represent a new and substantial advance towards these aims;

Having taken into consideration the decisions of the London Conference as set out in the Final Act of October 3, 1954, and its Annexes;

Have appointed as their Plenipotentiaries:

His Majesty the King of the Belgians
His Excellency M. Paul-Henri Spaak, Minister
of Foreign Affairs.

The President of the French Republic, President
of the French Union
His Excellency M. Pierre Mendès-France, Prime
Minister, Minister of Foreign Affairs.

The President of the Federal Republic of Germany
His Excellency Dr. Konrad Adenauer, Federal
Chancellor, Federal Minister of Foreign Affairs.

The President of the Italian Republic
His Excellency M. Gaetano Martino, Minister of
Foreign Affairs.

Her Royal Highness the Grand Duchess of
Luxembourg
His Excellency M. Joseph Bech, Prime Minister,
Minister of Foreign Affairs.

Her Majesty the Queen of the Netherlands
His Excellency M. Johan Willem Beyen, Minister
of Foreign Affairs.

Her Majesty The Queen of the United Kingdom of
Great Britain and Northern Ireland and of Her
other Realms and Territories, Head of the
Commonwealth
For the United Kingdom of Great Britain and
Northern Ireland
The Right Honourable Sir Anthony Eden, KG,
MC, Member of Parliament, Principal Secretary
of State for Foreign Affairs.

Who, having exhibited their full powers found in good and due form,

Have agreed as follows:

ARTICLE I

The Federal Republic of Germany and the Italian Republic hereby
accede to the Treaty as modified and completed by the present Protocol.

The High Contracting Parties to the present Protocol consider the
Protocol on Forces of Western European Union (hereinafter referred to
as Protocol No. II), the Protocol on the Control of Armaments and its
Annexes (hereinafter referred to as Protocol No. III), and the Protocol
on the Agency of Western European Union for the Control of Armaments
(hereinafter referred to as Protocol No. IV) to be an integral part of the
present Protocol.

ARTICLE II

The sub-paragraph of the preamble to the Treaty: "to take such steps as may be held necessary in the event of renewal by Germany of a policy of aggression" shall be modified to read: "to promote the unity and to encourage the progressive integration of Europe".

The opening words of the second paragraph of Article I shall read: "The co-operation provided for in the preceding paragraph, which will be effected through the Council referred to in Article VIII ...".

ARTICLE III

The following new Article shall be inserted in the Treaty as Article IV: "In the execution of the Treaty the High Contracting Parties and any organs established by Them under the Treaty shall work in close co-operation with the North Atlantic Treaty Organisation.

Recognising the undesirability of duplicating the military staffs of NATO, the Council and its Agency will rely on the appropriate military authorities of NATO for information and advice on military matters".

Articles IV, V, VI and VII of the Treaty will become respectively Articles V, VI, VII and VIII.

ARTICLE IV

Article VIII of the Treaty (formerly Article VII) shall be modified to read as follows:

"1. For the purposes of strengthening peace and security and of promoting unity and of encouraging the progressive integration of Europe and closer co-operation between Them and with other European organisations, the High Contracting Parties to the Brussels Treaty shall create a Council to consider matters concerning the execution of this Treaty and of its Protocols and their Annexes.

2. This Council shall be known as the 'Council of Western European Union'; it shall be so organised as to be able to exercise its functions continuously; it shall set up such subsidiary bodies as may be considered necessary: in particular, it shall establish immediately an Agency for the Control of Armaments whose functions are defined in Protocol No. IV.

3. At the request of any of the High Contracting Parties the Council shall be immediately convened in order to permit Them to consult with

regard to any situation which may constitute a threat to peace, in whatever area this threat should arise, or a danger to economic stability.

4. The Council shall decide by unanimous vote questions for which no other voting procedure has been or may be agreed. In the cases provided for in Protocols II, III and IV it will follow the various voting procedures, unanimity, two-thirds majority, simple majority, laid down therein. It will decide by simple majority questions submitted to it by the Agency for the Control of Armaments".

ARTICLE V

A new Article shall be inserted in the Treaty as Article IX: "The Council of Western European Union shall make an annual report on its activities and in particular concerning the control of armaments to an Assembly composed of representatives of the Brussels Treaty Powers to the Consultative Assembly of the Council of Europe".

The Articles VIII, IX and X of the Treaty shall become respectively Articles X, XI and XII.

ARTICLE VI

The present Protocol and other Protocols listed in Article I above shall be ratified and the instruments of ratification shall be deposited as soon as possible with the Belgian Government.(1)

They shall enter into force when all instruments of ratification of the present Protocol have been deposited with the Belgian Government and the instruments of accession of the Federal Republic of Germany to the North Atlantic Treaty have been deposited with the Government of the United States of America.(2)

The Belgian Government shall inform the Governments of the other High Contracting Parties and the Government of the United States of America of the deposit of each instrument of ratification.

In witness whereof the above-mentioned Plenipotentiaries have signed the present Protocol and have affixed thereto their seals.

---

(1) RATIFICATIONS   Date of deposit

Italy .... April 20, 1955
Belgium .... April 22, 1955
Netherlands .... May 1, 1955
Luxembourg .... May 4, 1955
France .... May 5, 1955
Federal Republic of Germany ..... May 5, 1955
United Kingdom .... May 5, 1955

(2) May 6, 1955

Done at Paris this twenty-third day of October, 1954, in two texts, in the English and French languages, each text being equally authoritative in a single copy which shall remain deposited in the archives of the Belgian Government and of which certified copies shall be transmitted by that Government to each of the other signatories.

For Belgium:
(L.S.) P.-H. SPAAK.
For France:
(L.S.) P. MENDÈS-FRANCE.
For the Federal Republic of Germany:
(L.S.) ADENAUER.
For Italy:
(L.S.) G. MARTINO.
For Luxembourg:
(L.S.) JOS. BECH.
For the Netherlands:
(L.S.) J. W. BEYEN.
For the United Kingdom of Great Britain and Northern Ireland:
(L.S.) ANTHONY EDEN.

(Annexes Ia, Ib, IIa, IIb are not reproduced).

PROTOCOL No. II ON FORCES OF
WESTERN EUROPEAN UNION
signed at Paris on October 23, 1954;
entered into force on May 6, 1955

His Majesty the King of the Belgians, the President of the French Republic, President of the French Union, the President of the Federal Republic of Germany, the President of the Italian Republic, Her Royal Highness the Grand Duchess of Luxembourg, Her Majesty the Queen of the Netherlands, and Her Majesty the Queen of the United Kingdom of Great Britain and Nothern Ireland and of Her other Realms and Territories, Head of the Commonwealth, Signatories of the Protocol Modifying and Completing the Brussels Treaty,

Having consulted the North Atlantic Council,

Have appointed as their Plenipotentiaries:

His Majesty the King of the Belgians
His Excellency M. Paul-Henri Spaak, Minister of Foreign Affairs.

The President of the French Republic, President of the
French Union
His Excellency M. Pierre Mendès-France, Prime Minister,
Minister of Foreign Affairs.

The President of the Federal Republic of Germany
His Excellency Dr. Konrad Adenauer, Federal Chancellor,
Federal Minister of Foreign Affairs.

The President of the Italian Republic
His Excellency M. Gaetano Martino, Minister of Foreign Affairs.

Her Royal Highness the Grand Duchess of Luxembourg
His Excellency M. Joseph Bech, Prime Minister, Minister
of Foreign Affairs.

Her Majesty the Queen of the Netherlands
His Excellency M. Johan Willem Beyen, Minister of Foreign Affairs.

Her Majesty The Queen of the United Kingdom of Great Britain and Northern Ireland and of Her other Realms and Territories, Head of the Commonwealth

For the United Kingdom of Great Britain and Northern Ireland The Right Honourable Sir Anthony Eden, KG, MC, Member of Parliament, Principal Secretary of State for Foreign Affairs.

Have agreed as follows:

ARTICLE I

1. The land and air forces which each of the High Contracting Parties to the present Protocol shall place under the Supreme Allied Commander, Europe, in peacetime on the mainland of Europe shall not exceed in total strength and number of formations:

(a) for Belgium, France, the Federal Republic of Germany, Italy and the Netherlands, the maxima laid down for peacetime in the Special Agreement annexed to the Treaty on the Establishment of a European Defence Community signed at Paris, on May 27, 1952; and

(b) for the United Kingdom, four divisions and the Second Tactical Air Force;

(c) for Luxembourg, one regimental combat team.

2. The number of formations mentioned in paragraph 1 may be brought up to date and adapted as necessary to make them suitable for the North Atlantic Treaty Organisation, provided that the equivalent fighting capacity and total strengths are not exceeded.

3. The statement of these maxima does not commit any of the High Contracting Parties to build up or maintain forces at these levels, but maintains their right to do so if required.

ARTICLE II

As regards naval forces, the contribution to NATO Commands of each of the High Contracting Parties to the present Protocol shall be determined each year in the course of the Annual Review (which takes into account the recommendations of the NATO military authorities). The naval forces of the Federal Republic of Germany shall consist of the vessels and formations necessary for the defensive missions assigned to it by the North Atlantic Treaty Organisation within the limits laid down in the Special Agreement mentioned in Article I, or equivalent fighting capacity.

ARTICLE III

If at any time during the Annual Review recommendations are put forward, the effect of which would be to increase the level of forces above the limits specified in Articles I and II, the acceptance by the country concerned of such recommended increases shall be subject to the unanimous approval of the High Contracting Parties to the present Protocol expressed either in the Council of Western European Union or in the North Atlantic Treaty Organisation.

ARTICLE IV

In order that it may establish that the limits specified in Articles I and II are being observed, the Council of Western European Union will regularly receive information acquired as a result of inspections carried out by the Supreme Allied Commander, Europe. Such information will be transmitted by a high-ranking officer designated for the purpose by the Supreme Allied Commander, Europe.

ARTICLE V

The strength and armaments of the internal defence and police forces on the mainland of Europe of the High Contracting Parties to the present Protocol shall be fixed by agreements within the Organisation of Western European Union, having regard to their proper functions and needs and to their existing levels.

ARTICLE VI

Her Majesty The Queen of the United Kingdom of Great Britain and Northern Ireland will continue to maintain on the mainland of Europe, including Germany, the effective strength of the United Kingdom forces which are now assigned to the Supreme Allied Commander, Europe, that is to say four divisions and the Second Tactical Air Force, or such other forces as the Supreme Allied Commander, Europe, regards as having equivalent fighting capacity. She undertakes not to withdraw these forces against the wishes of the majority of the High Contracting Parties who should take their decision in the knowledge of the views of the Supreme Allied Commander, Europe. This undertaking shall not, however, bind her in the event of an acute overseas emergency. If the maintenance of the United Kingdom forces on the mainland of Europe throws at any time too great a strain on the external finances of the United Kingdom, she will, through Her Government in the United Kingdom of Great Britain and Northern Ireland, invite the North Atlantic Council to review the financial conditions on which the United Kingdom formations are maintained.

In witness whereof, the above-mentioned Plenipotentiaries have signed the present Protocol, being one of the Protocols listed in Article I of the Protocol modifying and completing the Treaty, and have affixed thereto their seals.

Done at Paris this twenty-third day of October, 1954, in two texts, in the English and French languages, each text being equally authoritative, in a single copy, which shall remain deposited in the archives of the Belgian Government and of which certified copies shall be transmitted by that Government to each of the other Signatories.

For Belgium:
    (L.S.) P.-H. SPAAK.

For France:
    (L.S.) P. MENDÈS-FRANCE.

For the Federal Republic of Germany:
    (L.S.) ADENAUER.

For Italy:
    (L.S.) G. MARTINO.

For Luxembourg:
    (L.S.) JOS. BECH.

For the Netherlands:
    (L.S.) J. W. BEYEN.

For the United Kingdom of Great Britain and Northern Ireland:
    (L.S.) ANTHONY EDEN.

(Protocols III and IV are not reproduced)

Appendix II
The Rome Declaration

1. At the invitation of the Italian Government, the Foreign and Defence Ministers of the seven member States of Western European Union met in extraordinary session in Rome on 26-27 October 1984 to mark the 30th anniversary of the modified Brussels Treaty.

2. The Ministers stressed the importance of the Treaty and their attachment to its goals:

— to strengthen peace and security,
— to promote the unity and to encourage the progressive integration of Europe,
— to co-operate more closely both among member States and with other European organisations.

3. Conscious of the continuing necessity to strengthen Western security and of the specifically Western European geographical, political, psychological and military dimensions, the Ministers underlined their determination to make better use of the W.E.U. framework in order to increase co-operation between the member States in the field of security policy and to encourage consensus. In this context, they called for continued efforts to preserve peace, strengthen deterrence and defence and thus consolidate stability through dialogue and co-operation.

4. The Ministers recalled that the Atlantic Alliance, which remains the foundation of Western security, had preserved peace on the Continent for 35 years. This permitted the construction of Europe. The Ministers are convinced that a better utilisation of W.E.U. would not only contribute to the security of Western Europe but also to an improvement in the common defence of all the countries of the Atlantic Alliance and to greater solidarity among its members.

5. The Ministers emphasised the indivisibility of security within the

North Atlantic Treaty area. They recalled in particular the vital and substantial contribution of all the European allies and underlined the crucial importance of the contribution to common security of their allies who are not members of W.E.U. They stressed the necessity, as a complement to their joint efforts, of the closest possible concertation with them.

6.   The Ministers are convinced that increased co-operation within W.E.U. will also contribute to the maintenance of adequate military strength and political solidarity and, on that basis, to the pursuit of a more stable relationship between the countries of East and West by fostering dialogue and co-operation.

7.   The Ministers called attention to the need to make the best use of existing resources through increased co-operation, and through W.E.U. to provide a political impetus to institutions of co-operation in the field of armaments.

8.   The Ministers therefore decided to hold comprehensive discussions and to seek to harmonise their views on the specific conditions of security in Europe, in particular:
   — defence questions,
   — arms control and disarmament,
   — the effects of developments in East-West relations on the security of Europe,
   — Europe's contribution to the strengthening of the Atlantic Alliance, bearing in mind the importance of transatlantic relations,
   — the development of European co-operation in the field of armaments in respect of which W.E.U. can provide a political impetus.
They may also consider the implications for Europe of crises in other regions of the world.

9.   The Ministers recalled the importance of the W.E.U. Assembly which, as the only European parliamentary body mandated by Treaty to discuss defence matters, is called upon to play a growing role.
   They stressed the major contribution which the Assembly has already made to the revitalisation of W.E.U. and called upon it to pursue its efforts to strengthen the solidarity among the member States, and to strive to consolidate the consensus among public opinion on their security and defence needs.

10. In pursuance of these goals, the Ministers have decided on a number of specific measures with regard to the better functioning of the W.E.U. structure and organisation, which are set out in a separate document.

Institutional Reform of W.E.U.

At their meeting in Rome on 26 and 27 October 1984 to mark the 30th anniversary of the modified Brussels Treaty of 1954, the Foreign and Defence Ministers of the signatory States decided to make fuller use of the institutions of W.E.U. and, accordingly, to bring the existing institutions into line with the changed tasks of the Organisation.

I. *Activation of the Council*

The Ministers regard activation of the Council as a central element in the efforts to make greater use of Western European Union. In conformity with Article VIII of the modified Brussels Treaty, which allows the Council to decide on the organisation of its work and to consult or set up subsidiary bodies, the Ministers decided the following:

1. The Council would in future normally meet twice a year at ministerial level. One of these sessions could take place in a small group with no formal agenda. These meetings would bring together the Foreign Ministers and Defence Ministers. Separate meetings of the Foreign Ministers and/or Defence Ministers could also take place if the member States considered it necessary, to discuss matters lying within their respective area of responsibility.

2. The Presidency of the Council will be held by each member State for a one year term. Meetings of the Council will in principle take place in the country holding the Presidency.

3. The work of the Permanent Council will have to be intensified in line with the increased activities of the Council of Ministers. The Permanent Council, mandated to discuss in greater detail the views expressed by the Ministers and to follow up their decisions, will, pursuant to the second paragraph of the above-mentioned Article VIII, make the necessary arrangements for this purpose, including as appropriate the setting-up of working groups.

4. The Secretariat-General should be adapted to take account of the enhanced activities of the Council of Ministers and the Permanent Council.

5. The Ministers have asked the Secretariat-General to submit, as soon as possible, a report on the work done by the Secretariat and to consider what measures might be necessary to strengthen its activities. In this connection, the Ministers stated that any reorganisation in the staffing of the Secretariat-General should take account of the adjustments made elsewhere in the other W.E.U. institutions. They stressed that any proposed adjustments should not result in an overall increase in the Organisation's establishment.

II. *Relations between Council and Assembly*

The Ministers supported the idea of greater contact between the Council and the Assembly.

Recalling that, under Article IX of the Treaty, the Assembly is expressly required to discuss the reports submitted to it by the Council of Ministers on matters concerning the security and defence of the member States, and considering that the practice adopted has enabled the Assembly to widen the topics of its discussions, the Ministers wish to see the Assembly playing an increasing role, particularly by contributing even more to associating public opinion in the member States with the policy statements of the Council, which expresses the political will of the individual governments. Accordingly, the Ministers submit the following proposals to the Assembly:

1. In order to improve the contacts between the Council and the Assembly, the Ministers believe there are a number of options, noteworthy among which are:

— A substantial improvement in the existing procedures for giving written replies to Assembly Recommendations and questions. On this point, the Ministers consider that a leading role should be given to the Presidency, making the best use of the services of the Secretariat-General.

— The development of informal contacts between government representatives and the representatives of the Assembly.

— If appropriate, a colloquium involving the Presidency of the Council and the Committees of the Assembly.

— The improvement of the contacts that traditionally take place after the ministerial meetings of the Council, and more generally, the improvement of the procedures under which the Assembly is kept informed by the Presidency, whose representatives could—between the Assembly sessions—keep the various committees up to date with the work of the Council and even take part in their discussions.

— The possibility that the Assembly might make use of contributions from the technical institutions of W.E.U.

2. Convinced that greater co-operation between the Council and the Assembly is a key factor in the enhanced utilisation of W.E.U., the Ministers underscored the importance they attach to the Recommendations and the work of the Assembly.

3. Without wishing to preempt the decision of the members of the Assembly, the Ministers also stress the value, in their eyes, of developing a dialogue between the Assembly and other parliaments or parliamentary institutions.

4. The Ministers also stated that the member States were always ready to inform their national delegations of their governments' attitude to questions dealt with in Assembly reports and were prepared to offer information to their rapporteurs.

III. *Agency for the Control of Armaments and the Standing Armaments Committee*

The Ministers also considered the activity of the Agency for the Control of Armaments (ACA) and the Standing Armaments Committee (SAC).

1. In connection with the Agency, which was set up in 1954 to monitor compliance with the voluntary arms limitations agreed by the contracting parties, the Ministers underlined the exemplary nature of these commitments, which had instilled confidence among the signatory States and for this reason they acclaimed the work that the Agency had done.

Noting the value of the experience thus gained, the Ministers emphasised the interest that they attached to the development by the W.E.U. member States of reflection on arms control and disarmament questions.

2. As regards the SAC, the Ministers recalled the importance of the tasks defined in the decision of the Council of 7 May 1955 which established this body.

In this connection, they emphasised that the existence of an effective and competitive European armaments industry was a fundamental aspect of Europe's contribution to the Atlantic Alliance. In this context, it seemed very important to them that the seven member States of W.E.U. should be able to harmonise their positions in this sphere and co-ordinate their efforts with a view to increasing the effectiveness of co-operative activity in the various multilateral fora.

3. With the aim of better adapting the institutions of W.E.U. to present and future requirements, the Ministers reached the following decisions.

a) Noting that the control functions originally assigned to the ACA have now become, for the most part, superfluous, the Ministers decided, in accordance with Article V of Protocol No. III, which allows the Council to make changes to the ACA's control activity, to abolish gradually the remaining quantitative controls on conventional weapons. The Ministers agreed that these controls should be substantially reduced by 1 January 1985 and entirely lifted by 1 January 1986. The commitments and controls concerning ABC weapons would be maintained at the existing level and in accordance with the procedures agreed up to the present time.

b) The Ministers have instructed the Permanent Council to define, in consultation with the directors of the ACA and the SAC, the precise modalities of an overall reorganisation affecting both the ACA, the International Secretariat of the SAC and the SAC which could be structured in such a way as to fulfil a threefold task:

— to study questions relating to arms control and disarmament whilst carrying out the remaining control functions;

— undertake the function of studying security and defence problems;

— to contribute actively to the development of European armaments co-operation.

c) As regards the first two functions indicated above the intention would be to have available a common basis of analysis which could form a useful point of reference for the work of both the Council and the Assembly and also for informing public opinion.

This reorganisation will have to be carried out taking into account, on the one hand, changes in duties resulting first from the reduction and then from the abolition of the control tasks and, on the other hand, the need to have the appropriate experts available.

d) As regards armaments co-operation, W.E.U. should be in a position to play an active role in providing political impetus:

— by supporting all co-operative efforts including those of the IEPG and the CNAD;

— by encouraging in particular the activity of the IEPG as a forum whose main objective is to promote European co-operation and also to contribute to the development of balanced co-operation within the Atlantic Alliance;

— by developing continuing concertation with the various existing bodies.

e) In this general context, the Permanent Council will also take into account the existence of the FINABEL framework.

f) In carrying out this overall reorganisation the Permanent Council will have to:

— propose a precise organisation table which will make it possible to define and give a breakdown of the posts required for carrying out the three functions referred to above;

— ensure that the various arrangements proposed remain within the present limits in terms of staff and the Organisation's budget, without weakening W.E.U.'s ability to play its role;

The Ministers asked the Permanent Council to complete its work before their next session. They expressed the wish, however, that in the meantime a start should be made on all or part of the new tasks as soon as possible.

IV. *Contacts with non-member States*

1. The Ministers also attached great importance to liaison with those States in the Alliance which are not members of W.E.U.

2. Invoking the relevant provisions of the modified Brussels Treaty, and in particular Article IV, the Ministers pointed out that it was the responsibility of the Presidency of W.E.U. to inform those countries on either a bilateral or multilateral basis.

Appendix III
The Platform on European
Security Interests
The Hague, 27 October 1987

1. Stressing the dedication of our countries to the principles upon which our democracies are based and resolved to preserve peace in freedom, we, the Foreign and Defence Ministers of the member States of WEU, reaffirm the common destiny which binds our countries.

2. We recall our commitment to build a European union in accordance with the Single European Act, which we all signed as members of the European Community. We are convinced that the construction of an integrated Europe will remain incomplete as long as it does not include security and defence.

3. An important means to this end is the modified Brussels Treaty. This Treaty with its far-reaching obligations to collective defence, marked one of the early steps on the road to European unification. It also envisages the progressive association of other States inspired by the same ideals and animated by the like determination. We see the revitalisation of WEU as an important contribution to the broader process of European unification.

4. We intend therefore to develop a more cohesive European defence identity which will translate more effectively into practice the obligations of solidarity to which we are committed through the modified Brussels and North Atlantic Treaties.

5. We highly value the continued involvement in this endeavour of the WEU Assembly which is the only European parliamentary body mandated by treaty to discuss all aspects of security including defence.

I. *Our starting point is the present conditions of European security*

1.   Europe remains at the centre of East-West relations and, forty years after the end of the Second World War, a divided continent. The human consequences of this division remain unacceptable, although certain concrete improvements have been made on a bilateral level and on the basis of the Helsinki Final Act. We owe it to our people to overcome this situation and to exploit in the interest of all Europeans the opportunities for further improvements which may present themselves.

2.   New developments in East-West relations, particularly in arms control and disarmament, and also other developments, for example in the sphere of technology, could have far-reaching implications for European security.

3.   We have not yet witnessed any lessening of the military build-up which the Soviet Union has sustained over so many years. The geostrategic situation of Western Europe makes it particularly vulnerable to the superior conventional, chemical and nuclear forces of the Warsaw Pact. This is the fundamental problem for European security. The Warsaw Pact's superior conventional forces and its capability for surprise attack and large-scale offensive action are of special concern in this context.

4.   Under these conditions the security of the Western European countries can only be ensured in close association with our North American allies. The security of the Alliance is indivisible. The partnership between the two sides of the Atlantic rests on the twin foundations of shared values and interests. Just as the commitment of the North American democracies is vital to Europe's security, a free, independent and increasingly more united Western Europe is vital to the security of North America.

5.   It is our conviction that the balanced policy of the Harmel Report remains valid. Political solidarity and adequate military strength within the Atlantic Alliance, arms control, disarmament and the search for genuine détente continue to be integral parts of this policy. Military security and a policy of détente are not contradictory but complementary.

II. *European security should be based on the following criteria*

1.   It remains our primary objective to prevent any kind of war. It is our purpose to preserve our security by maintaining defence readiness and military capabilities adequate to deter aggression and intimidation without seeking military superiority.

2.   In the present circumstances and as far as we can foresee, there is no alternative to the Western strategy for the prevention of war, which has ensured peace in freedom for an unprecedented period of European history. To be credible and effective, the strategy of deterrence and defence must continue to be based on an adequate mix of appropriate nuclear and conventional forces, only the nuclear element of which can confront a potential aggressor with an unacceptable risk.

3.   The substantial presence of US conventional and nuclear forces plays an irreplaceable part in the defence of Europe. They embody the American commitment to the defence of Europe and provide the indispensable linkage with the US strategic deterrent.

4.   European forces play an essential role: the overall credibility of the Western strategy of deterrence and defence cannot be maintained without a major European contribution, not least because the conventional imbalance affects the security of Western Europe in a very direct way.

The Europeans have a major responsibility both in the field of conventional and nuclear defence. In the conventional field, the forces of the WEU member States represent an essential part of those of the Alliance. As regards nuclear forces, all of which form a part of deterrence, the co-operative arrangements that certain member States maintain with the United States are necessary for the security of Europe. The independent forces of France and the United Kingdom contribute to overall deterrence and security.

5.   Arms control and disarmament are an integral part of Western security policy and not an alternative to it. They should lead to a stable balance of forces at the lowest level compatible with our security. Arms control policy should, like our defence policy, take into account the specific European security interests in an evolving situation. It must be consistent with the maintenance of the strategic unity of the Alliance and should not preclude closer European defence co-operation. Arms

control agreements have to be effectively verifiable and stand the test of time. East and West have a common interest in achieving this.

III   *The Member States of WEU intend to assume fully their responsibilities:*

a.   *In the field of Western defence*

1.   We recall the fundamental obligation of Article V of the modified Brussels Treaty to provide all the military and other aid and assistance in our power in the event of armed attack on any one of us. This pledge, which reflects our common destiny, reinforces our commitments under the Atlantic Alliance, to which we all belong, and which we are resolved to preserve.

2.   It is our conviction that a more united Europe will make a stronger contribution to the Alliance, to the benefit of Western security as a whole. This will enhance the European role in the Alliance and ensure the basis for a balanced partnership across the Atlantic. We are resolved to strengthen the European pillar of the Alliance.

3.   We are each determined to carry our share of the common defence in both the conventional and the nuclear field, in accordance with the principles of risk- and burden-sharing which are fundamental to allied cohesion.

   — In the conventional field, all of us will continue to play our part in the on-going efforts to improve our defences;
   — In the nuclear field also, we shall continue to carry our share: some of us by pursuing appropriate co-operative arrangements with the US; the UK and France by continuing to maintain independent nuclear forces, the credibility of which they are determined to preserve.

4.   We remain determined to pursue European integration including security and defence and make a more effective contribution to the common defence of the West.

   To this end we shall:

   — ensure that our determination to defend any member country at its borders is made clearly manifest by means of appropriate arrangements,

— improve our consultations and extend our co-ordination in defence and security matters and examine all practical steps to this end,
— make the best possible use of the existing institutional mechanisms to involve the defence ministers and their representatives in the work of WEU,
— see to it that the level of each country's contribution to the common defence adequately reflects its capabilities,
— aim at a more effective use of existing resources, inter alia by expanding bilateral and regional military co-operation, pursue our efforts to maintain in Europe a technologically advanced industrial base and intensify armaments co-operation,
— concert our policies on crises outside Europe in so far as they may affect our security interests.

5. Emphasizing the vital contribution of the non WEU members of the Alliance to the common security and defence, we will continue to keep them informed of our activities.

b. *In the field of arms control and disarmament*

1. We shall pursue an active arms control and disarmament policy aimed at influencing future developments in such a way as to enhance security and to foster stability and co-operation in the whole of Europe. The steadfastness and cohesion of the Alliance and close consultations among all the Allies remain essential if concrete results are to be brought about.

2. We are committed to elaborate further our comprehensive concept of arms control and disarmament in accordance with the Alliance's declaration of 12 June 1987 and we will work within the framework of this concept as envisaged particularly in paragraphs 7 and 8 of this declaration. An agreement between the US and the Soviet Union for the global elimination of land-based INF missiles with a range between 500 and 5500 km will constitute an important element of such an approach.

3. In pursuing such an approach we shall exploit all opportunities to make further progress towards arms reductions, compatible with our security and with our priorities, taking into account the fact that work in this area raises complex and interrelated issues. We shall evaluate them together, bearing in mind the political and military requirements of our security and progress in the different negotiations.

c. *In the field of East-West dialogue and co-operation*

1. The common responsibility of all Europeans is not only to preserve the peace but to shape it constructively. The Helsinki Final Act continues to serve as our guide to the fulfilment of the objective of gradually overcoming the division of Europe. We shall therefore continue to make full use of the CSCE process in order to promote comprehensive co-operation among all participating states.

2. The possibilities contained in the Final Act should be fully exploited. We therefore intend:

— to seek to increase the transparency of military potentials and activities and the calculability of behaviour in accordance with the Stockholm Document of 1986 by further confidence-building measures.
— vigorously to pursue our efforts to provide for the full respect of human rights without which no genuine peace is possible.
— to open new mutually beneficial possibilities in the fields of economy, technology, science and the protection of the environment.
— to achieve more opportunities for the people in the whole of Europe to move freely and to exchange opinions and information and to intensify cultural exchanges, and thus to promote concrete improvements for the benefit of all people in Europe.

It is our objective to further European integration. In this perspective we will continue our efforts towards closer security co-operation, maintaining coupling with the United States and ensuring conditions of equal security in the Alliance as a whole.

We are conscious of the common heritage of our divided continent, all the people of which have an equal right to live in peace and freedom. That is why we are determined to do all in our power to achieve our ultimate goal of a just and lasting peaceful order in Europe.

Appendix IV
Documents Relating to the Enlargement of WEU to Portugal and Spain

PROTOCOL

for the accession of the Portuguese Republic and the Kingdom of Spain to the Treaty of Economic, Social and Cultural Collaboration and Collective Self-Defence, signed at Brussels on 17th March 1948, as amended by the 'Protocol modifying and completing the Brussels Treaty', signed at Paris on 23 October 1954

The parties to the Treaty of Economic, Social and Cultural Collaboration and Collective Self-Defence signed at Brussels on 17th March 1948, as modified and completed by the Protocol signed at Paris on 23rd October 1954 and the other protocols and annexes which form an integral part thereof, hereinafter referred to as 'the Treaty', on the one hand,

and the Portuguese Republic and Kingdom of Spain, on the other,

Reaffirming the common destiny which binds their countries and recalling their commitment to build a European union in accordance with the Single European Act;

Convinced that the construction of an integrated Europe will remain incomplete as long as it does not include security and defence;

Determined to develop a more cohesive European defence identity which will translate more effectively into practice the obligations of solidarity contained in the Treaty and in the North Atlantic Treaty;

Noting that the Portuguese Republic and the Kingdom of Spain, which are fully committed to the process of European construction and are members of the Atlantic Alliance, have formally stated that they are prepared to accede to the Treaty;

Noting that these two states accept unreservedly and in their entirety the Rome declaration of 27 October 1984 and the platform on European security interests adopted in The Hague on 27 October 1987 and that they are prepared to participate fully in their implementation;

Recalling the invitation issued on 19 April 1988 by the Council of Ministers of Western European Union to the Portuguese Republic and the Kingdom of Spain to open discussions with a view to their possible accession to the Treaty;

Noting the satisfactory conclusion of the discussions which followed this invitation;

Noting that the Portuguese Republic and the Kingdom of Spain have acknowledged the agreements, resolutions, decisions and rules of whatever nature adopted in the framework of Western European Union in conformity with the provisions of the Treaty;

Noting the invitation to accede to the Treaty issued to the Portuguese Republic and to the Kingdom of Spain on 14th November 1988;

Noting the political declaration adopted on 14th November 1988;

Considering that the enlargement of Western European Union to include the Portuguese Republic and the Kingdom of Spain represents a significant step in the development of European solidarity in the field of security and defence;

Have agreed as follows:

Article I

By the present Protocol, the Portuguese Republic and the Kingdom of Spain accede to the Treaty.

Article II

By their accession to the Treaty, the Portuguese Republic and the Kingdom of Spain become parties to the agreements concluded between the member states in fulfilment of the Treaty, listed by way of annex to the present Protocol.

Article III

Each of the signatory states shall notify the Belgian Government of the acceptance, approval or ratification of the present Protocol, which shall enter into force on the day of the receipt of the last of these notifications. The Belgian Government shall inform the signatory states of each such notification and of the entry into force of the Protocol.

In witness whereof the undersigned, being duly authorised thereto, have signed the present Protocol.

Done at London this fourteenth day of November, 1988, in two texts, in the English and French languages, each text being equally authoritative, in a single copy which shall remain deposited in the archives of the Belgian Government and certified copies of which shall be transmitted by that government to each of the other signatories.

For the Government of the Kingdom of Belgium:

For the Government of the French Republic:

For the Government of the Federal Republic of Germany:

For the Government of the Italian Republic:

For the Government of the Grand Duchy of Luxembourg:

For the Government of the Kingdom of the Netherlands:

For the Government of the Portuguese Republic:

For the Government of the Kingdom of Spain:

For the Government of the United Kingdom of Great Britain and Northern Ireland:

ANNEX

Agreements concluded between the member states in fulfilment of the Treaty:

1. Agreement on the status of Western European Union, national representatives and international staff, signed at Paris on 11th May 1955.

2. Agreement drawn up in implementation of Article V of Protocol No. II to the Treaty, signed at Paris on 14th December 1957.

242115

POLITICAL DECLARATION RELATING TO THE ENLARGEMENT OF WESTERN EUROPEAN UNION TO INCLUDE PORTUGAL AND SPAIN

During the consultations which were held with a view to the enlargement of WEU to include Portugal and Spain, the member states of WEU with Portugal and Spain, taking into consideration the spirit in which their security co-operation has recently developed, found that a number of the provisions of the Brussels Treaty, as modified in 1954, did not correspond to the way in which they intend to pursue and strengthen that co-operation, on the basis of the Rome declaration on 27th October 1984 and of the platform on European security interests, adopted in The Hague on 27th October 1987.

Consequently, the member states of WEU with Portugal and Spain consider that the relevant provisions of the Brussels Treaty, as modified in 1954, and its corresponding protocols will be re-examined, as appropriate, having regard for the practice and achievements of, and the prospects for, their co-operation in security matters.

TEXTS FOR EXCHANGE OF LETTERS ON ARTICLE X OF THE MODIFIED BRUSSELS TREATY

A.   Draft letter from Spanish Minister to each member state and Portugal

"Your Excellency,

I have the honour to refer to the Protocol signed this day for the accession of the Portuguese Republic and the Kingdom of Spain to the Treaty of Economic, Social and Cultural Collaboration and Collective Self-Defence, signed at Brussels on 17th March 1948, as amended by the protocol modifying and completing the Brussels Treaty, signed at Paris on 23rd October 1954, and to communicate the following in connection with Article X of the said Treaty, hereinafter referred to as 'the Treaty'.

The Government of the Kingdom of Spain proposes in this connection that the Kingdom of Spain shall not, as a consequence of its accession to the Treaty, be obliged to submit to the International Court of Justice, without its consent, any dispute between Spain and another party to the Treaty existing prior to the entry into force of the Treaty for Spain or relating to facts or situations existing before that date.

I should be grateful if Your Excellency would confirm that your

Government is in agreement with the above and that the exchange of letters thus effected will be considered as an annex to the protocol of accession, which will enter into force simultaneously therewith.

(formal close)"

*B. Draft reply from each member state and Portugal
   to the Spanish Minister*

"Your Excellency,

I have the honour to acknowledge receipt of your communication of today's date referring to the Protocol for the accession of the Portuguese Republic and the Kingdom of Spain to the Treaty of Economic, Social and Cultural Collaboration and Collective Self-Defence, signed at Brussels on 17th March 1948, as amended by the protocol modifying and completing the Brussels Treaty, signed at Paris on 23rd October 1954 and in particular to Article X of the said Treaty, hereinafter referred to as 'the Treaty'.

I have the honour in reply to confirm that, in the view of my Government, the Kingdom of Spain shall not, as a consequence of its accession to the Treaty, be obliged to submit to the International Court of Justice, without its consent, any dispute between Spain and another party to the Treaty existing prior to the entry into force of the Treaty for Spain or relating to facts or situations existing before that date, and that the present exchange of letters will be considered as an annex to the protocol of accession, which will enter into force simultaneously therewith.

(formal close)"

Appendix V
Collective Security:
The European Community and
the Preservation of Peace
By Michael Welsh, MEP

*Based on a paper by the European Democratic Group
of the European Parliament*

The Reykjavík meeting between President Reagan and General Secretary
Gorbachev inaugurated a new era in superpower relations, the signing
of the INF Treaty in Washington being its first concrete manifestation.
The basic assumptions which have underpinned defence policy in
Europe for the past decade can no longer be taken for granted and the
need for concertation between the European allies has never been more
obvious. As the French Minister for Defence, André Giraud, observed,
"Gorbachev has succeeded in raising the issue of European security to
the top of the international agenda".

Unfortunately, the change in strategic perceptions has plunged Western
Governments into considerable disarray. While there is a general desire
for a coherent policy on defence and security entitling the Europeans
to at least a ring-side seat at superpower negotiations, there is much
confusion as to the content of this policy and how it should be expressed.
Some states, notably the United Kingdom, continue to place a major
emphasis on the relationship with the United States as the guarantor of
European security; others, such as France, appear to regard the US as
less dependable and put their faith in a free-standing European pillar
within NATO. Britain and France regard an independent deterrent as
central to European security; others in the smaller countries and
Germany look for the rapid de-nuclearisation of Europe under an
American-based nuclear umbrella. France and Spain remain outside

the NATO command structure, Ireland is neutral, and Greece under a Socialist Government frequently gives the impression of being closer to the non-aligned countries than to her NATO partners. Certainly, there has been some success in relaunching WEU: the Hague Platform produced in October 1987 has been widely welcomed, and both Spain and Portugal have recently been admitted as new members. However, there is considerable doubt as to how these principles can be given practical effect and a widespread feeling that the WEU remains an excuse for not having a common defence policy rather than a means of producing one.

Underlying these differences of opinion is the threat that public opinion throughout Europe and particularly in Germany may not be willing to tolerate a nuclear-based strategy much longer or approve the increased spending on conventional forces which a reduced emphasis on nuclear deterrence would make necessary. Although the INF Treaty has exposed the fallacies at the heart of unilateralism, public expectations have been raised. The danger now is that the disarmament process will acquire its own momentum leading ineluctably to the demilitarisation of Western Europe which would be left hopelessly vulnerable to Soviet blackmail. European opinion must be convinced that a viable defence policy is a necessary element to preserve the democratic freedoms that characterise our societies. Demilitarisation, far from preserving our way of life, would end by destroying it.

Our policies rest on two assumptions. First, that the Soviet Union, Glasnost and Perestroika notwithstanding, will continue to constitute a potential threat. This threat is not necessarily one of invasion or nuclear attack, but of military superiority which, if conceded, might lead Western European countries to yield to diplomatic pressure in particular matters or situations, not only in Europe but also around the rest of the world. Second, that continued US involvement in European defence will be conditional on the willingness of Europeans to take an increasing share of the responsibility for defending themselves. As Margaret Thatcher said in her speech of 20 September 1988 in Bruges, "We must strive to maintain the US commitment to Europe's defence. That means recognising the burden on their resources of the world role they undertake and their point that their Allies should play a full part in the defence of freedom, particularly as Europe grows wealthier. Increasingly they will look to Europe to play a part in out-of-area defence, as we have recently done in the Gulf."

Given the size of the conventional gap, it is clear that deterrence through mutually-assured destruction (MAD) must remain at the heart of defensive strategy. The INF Treaty however raises serious questions over the viability of the accompanying doctrine of flexible response and a review at the highest NATO level is urgently necessary to ascertain how far flexible response can be preserved in post-INF Europe. The French and British independent strategic deterrents have a crucial role to play in maintaining the ultimate nuclear guarantee, and co-operation as regards targeting and scheduling of submarine patrols is very much to be welcomed; such co-operation cannot act as a substitute for an overall strategic plan, which to some extent at least takes the pressure off West Germany by providing some kind of additional intermediate tier. The details of such a plan are matters for military and defence experts but they need clear political directives.

WEU is the natural forum for working out such political guidelines. Indeed, useful progress has been made already in the shape of the Hague Platform. Although nine out of the twelve members of the Community and the fourteen European members of NATO belong to WEU, its political role and its relationships with other institutions such as European Political Co-operation (EPC) remain obscure. If the WEU is to provide the necessary impetus to the development of NATO's European pillar, it must be more than a talking shop, but not impinge on NATO's integrated command structure. There seems no good reason why a relationship could not be developed between EPC and the WEU, bearing in mind that proper account would need to be taken of the interests of those Europeran members of NATO which are not members of the European Communities. Such an arrangement would make it much easier for NATO Governments in countries such as Denmark to play a part in the development of European security policy without compromising themselves in the eyes of domestic public opinion and it would avoid fears of the biggest powers establishing some kind of defence hegemony at the expense of the smaller. Most important of all, it would enhance the political weight of WEU vis-à-vis the Americans and counter tendencies to conclude independent bilateral arrangements among the larger member states. At a recent meeting in

Paris, François Fillon, then Chairman of the Defence Committee of the French National Assembly, said "I prefer bilateral agreements to no agreements at all; trilateral is better than bilateral, four parties are better than three and so on". If we wish to avoid the fragmentation of defence policy in Europe we need to utilise existing institutions which bring all the parties together.

The ability of the European allies to equip themselves with an adequate range of military hardware is central to containing the conventional arms gap and developing a suitable response to the continuing Soviet threat. A European armaments industry capable of meeting European needs is essential if Europeans are going to have a credible presence in disarmament negotiations, and public acceptance of increased defence spending is far more likely if this results directly in additional job opportunities in Europe and enhancement of Europe's technological base. The failure to generate a common procurement policy must rank high among Europe's failures up to now. But the programme for completion of the internal market by 1992 and moves to liberalise public purchasing may offer a new opportunity to make one work. Essential components are an agreement on basic specifications currently covered by the Independent European Programme Group (IEPG)—a natural field of operation for WEU—and an agreement among the member states on subsidisation and state support for military research and development. If this could be achieved, perhaps using the framework of existing competition policy, it would be possible for the various staffs to shop around for the most competitive product within predetermined specifications, rather than being tied to national champions. This would make for a far more competitive and cost-effective arms industry than at present and would be likely to lead to an increasing degree to specialisation among the major producers and consequently more consortium-style bids for the biggest contracts. A common procurement policy is essential for a common security policy and neither is possible without common institutions.

In a speech to the Assembly of the Western European Union, the British Minister, David Mellor, said, "As the only European public forum specifically for security discussions your function must be closely tied to the need to develop public understanding of the major security and defence issues. ... This involves dialogue with governments: it means providing critiques for our policies so we keep up to the mark. And it will inevitably involve interpreting and explaining to public opinion the significance and meaning of some of the exchanges that occur".

Many of us in the European Parliament, however, feel that the latter, directly elected and made up of members specialising actively and continuously in European issues, is potentially better equipped to identify the basic political consensus necessary if a common security policy is to be forged. If a defence dimension to Community competence were added along the lines set out above, the Parliament would become the natural successor of the WEU Assembly and be enabled to play a crucial role in mobilising public support for European defence. As previously noted, there is a universal concern in all countries that such support cannot be taken for granted and the present arrangements have failed significantly in this respect. As Margaret Thatcher has said, "It is a question of political will and political courage, of convincing people in all our countries that we cannot rely for ever on others for our defence but that each Member of the Alliance must shoulder a fair share of the burden".

In the second paragraph of the Hague Platform, the Governments of the countries belonging to WEU declared:

"We recall our commitment to build a European Union in accordance with the Single European Act which we all signed as members of the European Community. We are convinced that the construction of an integrated Europe will remain incomplete as long as it does not include security and defence".

For years now, advocates of European Union have been disturbed by their palpable failure to capture public imagination and recreate the dynamic forces that led to the signing of the original treaties. The experience of the 1980s suggests that economics is not enough to justify European integration: people need a more powerful motivator. Adding defence and security to the range of Community activities could offer the European electorate an idea that was both orthodox in terms of the Hague Platform and fresh in that it would show the electorate that our vision of the Commmunity included the key question of the survival of our democracies through collective security and defence. In so doing we would be able to draw on the vast reserves of public support for adequate defence and clearly differentiate ourselves from those who have tended to see European Union as essentially neutralist.

Two policy statements follow. The first, printed in full, adopted in London in June 1988, was drawn up by the European Democratic Group in the European Parliament. The Group has 66 members drawn from the British and Danish Conservative Parties and the Spanish Alianza Popular. The statement underlines and demonstrates the extent of common ground on security issues between three parties who, although they share a common political philosophy, approach such issues from very different standpoints and against quite different domestic political backgrounds. The second statement, adopted in Rhodes in September 1988, was drawn up by a Committee of the European Democrat Union. The EDU is a confederation of Conservative and Christian Democratic parties, including many from countries which are members of neither NATO nor the European Community, and the statement was adopted by the leaders of those parties. The European Democratic Group has observer status within EDU. Again, the statement is proof that there is—at least amongst European political parties of the Centre-Right—enough common ground upon which to build a European pillar within the Atlantic Alliance and a real determination that Europe should assume greater responsibility for her own defence. For reasons of space only the second part of the statement, coming from the NATO member countries' EDU party leaders, has been included.

POLICY STATEMENT ADOPTED BY THE
European Democratic Group, London, June 1988

Principles

The essential object of a security policy is the prevention of war through the deterrence of aggression. For deterrence to be credible and thereby effective two basic conditions must be met: capacity for retaliation must be of sufficient strength to deter a potential aggressor; and the aggressor must believe that such a retaliation would actually take place.

The deterrence of aggression can best be achieved by a triple-pronged policy combining adequate defence; mutual, balanced and verifiable disarmament; and a continued policy of détente.

For the foreseeable future, collective security in Western Europe should be undertaken within the framework of the Atlantic Alliance. Any weakening of the Alliance would damage the credibility of our willingness and capacity to retaliate.

Disarmament can only be envisaged if it leads to a stable balance of forces, and ideally this should be achieved at the lowest level compatible with Western security.

Policy

The Atlantic Alliance should rest upon the twin pillars of the United States and Europe. The European pillar must be strengthened in a way which neither damages the cohesiveness of the Alliance, nor weakens the American commitment to the defence of Europe.

All Member States of the Community are bound by the Treaty of Rome and the Single European Act to establish "an ever closer Union". In October 1987 the seven Members of Western European Union* declared that "the construction of an integrated Europe will remain incomplete as long as it does not include security and defence". The Group supports this view.

Effective and credible deterrence in Europe can only be based on a combination of nuclear and conventional forces, because only nuclear forces can confront an aggressor enjoying superiority in conventional forces with an unacceptable degree of risk. The presence of US conventional and nuclear forces in Europe has hitherto played an essential part in the defence of Europe.

The effect of the INF Treaty is to remove all land-based nuclear forces from continental Western Europe other than short-range forces not capable of reaching the Soviet Union. Taken in conjunction with the manner in which the INF agreement was concluded between the USA and the Soviet Union, this development has two principal consequences:

---

* Belgium, France, Luxembourg, Italy, the Netherlands, the United Kingdom, West Germany.

(i) it makes a review of the strategy for the defence of Europe absolutely essential;

(ii) it underlines the importance of Western European countries assuming more responsibility for their own defence as the price for a continuing American commitment.

Such a review can only be carried out, and the conclusions applied, on the basis of adequate political guidelines. Western European Union is the natural forum for the development of such guidelines, and the Hague Platform represents a useful point of departure. The deficiencies of WEU could be overcome if there were a closer identification between membership of the Community and membership of WEU.

A common policy for the procurement and manufacture of defence equipment is a necessary concomitant of a common security policy. Defence procurement should be liberalised as part of the programme to complete the single market, along with other forms of public procurement. Such a development would require an extension of competition policy to cover subsidies to arms manufacturers and Government support of military research and development. However, we accept that true interchangeability and economies of scale will only be achieved when Member States adopt generally common and relatively simple designs with limited adaptations to meet different requirements.

It would be the Commission's responsibility to ensure that competition rules were observed within the framework of Articles 90-92 of the Treaty, for those products not covered by Article 225. The list of exempt products required by that Article should be drawn up as soon as possible.

Responsibility for specifying equipment requirements and procurement decisions would remain with the national authorities who are linked in IEPG.

The 1981 London agreement established the competence of European Political Co-operation to discuss security policy. It would be logical for the seven members of WEU to reflect the conclusions reached in EPC in their separate deliberations: this is a natural way for Member States who are not WEU members to make an input where their particular interests are concerned. The European Parliament is the only directly-elected institution where defence and security issues are regularly discussed. Consequently it has an important role to play in establishing a political consensus necessary to secure popular acceptance for defence and security policy. Where such a consensus can be established it must have a significant bearing on decisions taken in WEU. The Group believes that the development and refinement of these natural institutional links can play an important part in establishing a common defence and security policy among the Member States.

Within Western Europe and within the Community there is scope for bilateral arrangements between countries wanting to co-operate in the defence field. However, Europe should avoid a proliferation of different organisations concerned with defence.

It is essential that the countries of Western Europe co-ordinate their policies in disarmament negotations. That co-ordination must cover all categories of weapons since an assessment of the balance between the forces of the Atlantic Alliance and those of the Warsaw Pact can only be made on the basis of the overall picture. Europeans cannot expect to be consulted until they have something to say.

If the emphasis in the defence of Western Europe is to shift in the direction of conventional forces, this has profound budgetary consequences which must be explained to the electorate. Indeed, as Europeans assume more responsibility for their own defence we must ensure that our policies, some of them likely to be unpopular, enjoy the support of public opinion. European elections represent an opportunity to restate not only the fundamental importance of defence but also the principles upon which it must be based.

POLICY STATEMENT ADOPTED BY THE
European Democratic Union, Rhodes, September 1988
Recommendations of the EDU Party Leaders in the field of
European Security and Arms Control
Party Leaders coming from NATO member countries

Resolve to strengthen the Atlantic Alliance, with the involvement of the United States of America in Europe and to counteract any attempt to decouple;

Are convinced of the necessity that Europeans unite to discuss collectively the issues of peace in freedom, security, and arms control in Europe, in order to build up an effective basis for really intensive consultations within the Alliance prior to any negotiation between East and West;

To this end believe that the time has come effectively to build the European pillar of defence in one or the other form, so that the ultimate objective of a European Security Union for all those who want to participate in such an effort can be reached;

Are determined that a common policy on arms procurement plays an essential role in the efforts to rationalise and strengthen Europe's defence capability;

Agree the suggestion that the Western European Union on the basis of its Security Charter of The Hague (1987) could become an important factor in renewing and reinforcing the European pillar of Western defence, if the necessary reshaping and restructuring of this organization could be effected;

Note that the seven members of WEU also participate in the European Political Co-operation and that therefore discussions on political and economic aspects of security in the framework of this co-operation will necessarily be reflected in the deliberations of the WEU;

Recognise that the directly-elected European Parliament regularly discusses political and economic aspects of security and believes this to be a useful means of establishing the necessary popular consensus for European Security;

Stress the importance that any such European pillar, be it in the framework of a strengthened Western European Union or any other organization, reinforces the overall important Atlantic Alliance, which is and will be the overall important and decisive organization for Western defence and security policy;

Underline the necessity for standardized production of armament within the Alliance;

Are convinced of the necessity further to develop the principles of The Hague platform with the aim of giving them greater substance;

Will take all necessary steps to develop a common position on security policy, strategy, arms limitation and arms control and on Europe's security problems beyond European territories;

Underlining that the Western European Union is open to all European countries, members of the Atlantic Alliance, willing to meet its binding obligations;

Welcome the continuing French-British conversations on nuclear weapons.

Index